Stop Trying to Fix Your

Learn to Rest in the Overcoming Power of the Spirit

Eddie Snipes

A book by:
Exchanged Life Discipleship

Copyright © 2015 by Eddie Snipes and
Exchanged Life Discipleship

http://www.exchangedlife.com

ISBN: 978-0692491874

Contact the author by visiting http://www.eddiesnipes.com or http://www.exchangedlife.com

Table of Contents

The Best Advice I've Never Heard

Not long ago I had a conversation with a man who was struggling with an addiction. I said, "I'm going to share something with you that I wish someone had shared with me. It's something you probably have never heard from the church. Stop trying to fix yourself. Stop trying to overcome your addiction." I then went on to explain the biblical principles of our promise that God will defeat our sins, and He can do so without human effort.

This truth was born out of my own testimony. I grew up in church, but before I became a believer, my flesh was already hooked on sinful addictions. Once I became a Christian, I thought it was my responsibility to defeat my addiction. When I couldn't, it created a lot of guilt and frustration. For my first twenty or more years of my Christian life, I promised God I would stop, but it was a promise I had no power to keep.

When I fell, I felt God's anger. I repented, begged for forgiveness, swore off my sins, and fell again. And again. And again. On rare occasions, I could hold out for a few months, but usually I would peak out in a day or so. Inevitably, I'd fall, then I would hide from God.

At church the preacher would proclaim, "Look at your sin. Surely your sins will find you out. God is angry at the wicked everyday, and if your life isn't right when you walk out of here, you might have an accident and find yourself standing before an angry God."

Let me prelude this book by saying this is not the gospel Jesus taught. Nor is it the gospel taught by the apostles. I examine this topic in detail in my book, The Revelation of Grace, so I won't go into all the details again here. But what I will say is that the Old Testament Law put man under condemnation. Those who are under that law are still under God's wrath, but in Christ we have escaped wrath.[1]

---

[1] Romans 5:9

The entire Old Testament is designed to reveal to man that righteousness is impossible by human effort. That's why the Bible calls the law 'our tutor that brings us to Christ', but once Christ has come, we are no longer under that tutor.[2]

The truth is, God was not angry when I fell back into sin. Grieved, but not angry. He was grieved because He is a loving Father who wants the best for His children. God is grieved when His children are entangled in that which is harming them. He is also grieved when the suffering child is told that their father rages at their weaknesses. Because I believed this lie, I hid in fear, when I could have found relief by obeying God's command found in **Hebrews 4:16**

Let us therefore come boldly to the throne of grace, that we may obtain mercy and find grace to help in time of need.

The throne of grace is not for those who get their life right for God. It is for those who need help and mercy when they are in need. When my addictions and sinful habits overtook me, I was in need. Because I was told that when God got ahold of me, He was going to take me behind the woodshed, I feared the throne of God. I was taught the throne was a place of judgment, instead of the place of comfort, relief, and help. It is the place where God's loving favor is unconditional, and not dependent upon my ability to be perfect. It's where God perfects me, not the place where human perfection is a prerequisite.

It's called the throne of grace for a reason. Grace means God's favor, which cannot be earned. Grace is unearned and unearnable favor, based on God's nature of love, not man's worthiness or performance. When you do not deserve it, God demonstrates His unconditional love by calling us to His throne, where He pours His favor upon us, and gives us the power of His Spirit to help us in our time of need.

Wrath is dead. It was destroyed in Christ. Anyone who receives Christ has already escaped wrath – even if they blow it. I want you to read and digest this amazing passage. **Isaiah 54:8-10**

---

[2] Galatians 3:24-25

⁸ With a little wrath I hid My face from you for a moment; But with everlasting kindness I will have mercy on you," Says the LORD, your Redeemer.

⁹ "For this *is* like the waters of Noah to Me; For as I have sworn That the waters of Noah would no longer cover the earth, So have I sworn That I would not be angry with you, nor rebuke you.

¹⁰ For the mountains shall depart And the hills be removed, But My kindness shall not depart from you, Nor shall My covenant of peace be removed," Says the LORD, who has mercy on you.

The waters of Noah is referring to the flood. Because the earth was filled with sin and corruption, God judged the world with a flood, but after that judgement, God swore an unbreakable oath, "I will never again destroy the earth with water." Look around the earth now. The earth is again filled with sin and corruption. Powerful men are doing exactly what they were doing in Noah's day. The powerful are oppressing the weak. The earth is filled with violence and bloodshed. The thoughts of men are again evil continually.

Watch the news and see if this isn't the case. Murder after murder is presented to the viewer. People are afraid to walk down the inner city streets. In many countries, people are kidnapped for money or murdered for no other reason than to make a statement. Millions of people were killed under communist countries, and hundreds of thousands of people are killed in wars by non-communist countries. As you read this, countless people are being persecuted and killed by those who think murder is an act of obedience to their religion.

We could go on and on, but it's clear that the earth today is just as deserving of the flood as Noah's day, but it doesn't happen. Why? Because God's covenant of promise was not conditional on man's righteousness. In the same way, God has given you and I the covenant of promise. Just as God's promise was certain to Noah, God's promise is certain to you. Even if you sin, God has sworn that

He will never again put you under His wrath. It isn't a matter of whether you deserve it or not. It is a matter of God's promise that was given through Christ.

Isaiah 53 is the reason we have the promise we read in Isaiah 54. Here is why God's wrath is no longer a part of your life. Look at **Isaiah 53:5-6**

> [5] But He *was* wounded for our transgressions, *He was* bruised for our iniquities; The chastisement for our peace *was* upon Him, And by His stripes we are healed.
> [6] All we like sheep have gone astray; We have turned, every one, to his own way; And the LORD has laid on Him the iniquity of us all.

The wrath against all sin – including your sin – was applied to Christ. If you are in Christ, the Bible says that you are saved from wrath through Him. To shore up that promise to us, we have the above promise in Isaiah 54 – God has made an unbreakable covenant, based on His unbreakable word, you cannot be under wrath again. Even if the mountains and hills are removed from the earth, God has promised to you that He will NEVER remove His kindness from you. It's a guarantee.

Because no one told me this, but instead preached the opposite, I fled from the one place where help is abundant. I should have been running to the throne room of God instead of fleeing from God.

This is true for you. God knows your weaknesses. When you fail, God isn't surprised or disappointed. He knew your mistakes before you were born, and He still committed His love to you. He did so with the promise that His love has the power to cover a multitude of sins.[3] Not only that, but God has given us His Spirit with the promise that the Holy Spirit will be our helper, our comforter, and the one who teaches us how to walk in God's love, where our perfection is imparted to us from God.

There are people who believe that grace is a license to sin, or that grace (aka hypergrace) will cause people to fall back into sin.

---

[3] Proverbs 10:12, 1 Peter 4:8

The opposite is true. Look no farther than the local church. Most churches teach wrath and law, believing it will create enough fear to keep people out of sin. But we don't see spiritual maturity emerging from fear-based teaching.

What we do see is hypocrisy and rollercoaster Christianity. People are constantly recommitting their lives to Christ, but falling back into old habits within a few days. Also, look at the scandals that have plagued the church over the last two or three decades. I can't think of an example of a preacher falling into adultery or other sexual taboo that wasn't preaching condemnation. Why doesn't it work? Because it can't work. This is affirmed in **Romans 7:5**

> For when we were in the flesh, the sinful passions which were aroused by the law were at work in our members to bear fruit to death.

The law arouses sinful passions? Yes, because in order to keep the law, our religious efforts are dependent upon us, and when we put the flesh in control, we are not in the Spirit. The flesh cannot make itself righteous. But the opposite is true. Look at this promise in **Galatians 5:16**

> I say then: Walk in the Spirit, and you shall not fulfill the lust of the flesh.

This also is a guarantee. It is not you who defeat sin. It is the Spirit that defeats sin. We'll get into this in detail as we go along.

In the following chapters, I'll be repetitive on some things, but this is because many of the most powerful truths go against what most people believe, and we need to drive home these truths.

How I wish someone had taught me these truths. I worked hard to defeat my addiction, and had zero success. But when I learned to walk in the Spirit, these things began falling away, and as I learned to stop trusting in my self-efforts, the flesh began losing power. Then addictions began slipping away, until they became a powerless memory.

When I tried to force my flesh into legalistic Christianity, my best efforts couldn't keep righteousness from slipping away. When

I learned to walk in grace by faith, nothing in the flesh can keep sin from slipping away. Through my best efforts, I couldn't keep my hold on righteousness; under grace, sin can't keep its hold on me!

This book contains the advice I have given to many others. It is what worked (and is working) in my life. Now my prayer is these truths will bring life to you. Stop fixing yourself. Become a receiver of grace and a truster in Christ. Then see what God has planned for your joy, peace, and success!

Discussion Questions

Define Grace.

Review Hebrews 4:16. Explain who is welcomed before God.

What is the purpose of the throne of God in the New Covenant?

Why does God point to the covenant He made for Noah to help us understand the covenant of grace?

When people sinned, did God revoke His promise to Noah?

When people sin, does God revoke His promise of grace?

Can a Christian fall back under God's wrath? Why or why not?

Does the fear of judgment create people who thrive in the Spirit? Explain your answer.

Read Romans 7:5 and Galatians 5:16. Why does the law stir up the flesh, but the Spirit suppresses it?

Which does the Bible say keeps sin in check, keeping the law or walking by grace?

Does the Bible teach that grace gives us the ability to do the law? Explain.

You are an Overcomer

Every person has life controlling issues. Some are more socially acceptable, while others are more destructive. Whether your life is hindered by insecurity, selfishness, and anger, or whether you are dominated by substance abuse, depression, or behavioral addictions, we are all broken vessels.

The reason we struggle is because we were created incomplete. The voids in your life are there by design, because you were created to be complete in the Lord. God has declared the following in **Colossians 2:9-10**

9 For in Him dwells all the fullness of the Godhead bodily;

10 and you are complete in Him, who is the head of all principality and power.

The problem is not your addiction. It is not the issues that hinder, or even plague your life. The problem is that you were designed to be complete in Christ, and if you try to fill the empty voids with anything other than perfect union with God, you'll spend more time trying to fill in the empty places than thriving in life.

People who have already received the life of Christ continue to struggle because of bad teaching and flawed theology. Most of us have been taught that if we can fix ourselves, God will be pleased with us. This is a lie. God DOES NOT reject you because you are flawed and sinful. God does not want you to fix yourself. God has already given the fix, and He will not permit us to fill in the gaps of our lives with religion, works, or any form of self-effort. Every form of human effort is a rejection of God's provision.

God will not reject us because we have filled our lives with sin, destructive behaviors, good works, or self-effort. God rejects all of these things, but does not reject us. God removes these things while accepting and welcoming us. He removes what isn't compatible with His perfect love. The burden is His, not ours.

We have to overcome two main lies. One lie is that God is pleased when we do enough to satisfy Him. The other is that God is angry at us because we have sinned.

God does not shake His head in disgust when we have destroyed our lives with sinful behaviors and bad choices. In fact, God delights in showing us that the more sin abounds, the more grace (God's unearned favor) abounds over sin.[4]

The truth is that light shines clearer in the darkness. Love is proven when it can't be deserved. The power of grace is revealed when it enters a sin-filled life. Grace drives sin out. It does not wait until sin is gone.

The reason we sin is because we have a lack in our lives, and we are tempted to fill that need by human effort. A person steals because they don't believe God can supply. A person lusts because the heart is not satisfied. Jealousy is because we fear loss. When there is a need inside, it is because our life is lacking. Temptation stops being tempting when there is no need. Consider the words of **Proverbs 27:7**

A satisfied soul loathes the honeycomb, But to a hungry soul every bitter thing *is* sweet.

When our souls are starving, bitter things appear sweet, and sin looks like something that should satisfy (which it can't). Where food is plenteous, people snub things they don't like, but where food is scarce, everything looks good. A starving man will eat from a dumpster, with no regard to sanitation or health. The same is true for a starving soul. Sin only appears sweet to the starving soul. Bitterness is cherished by the famished soul. Anger, jealousy, depression, and all self-focused and self-destructive behaviors are desired by a soul that is in want.

Our negative emotions and fleshly ways of thinking are the unhealthy cravings of our soul. Why does someone throw a pity-party? It is the soul relishing the opportunity to feed on negative emotions. No one is forcing us to brood. It is a willing feast on the things that a healthy soul would loathe.

---

[4] Romans 5:20

Because we are often taught to deal with problems and religion from the human perspective, we are actually starving our souls instead of feeding it. We are living off spiritual junk food.

Someone can satiate their hunger with chips and candy, but will they ever nourish their bodies? Our bodies can endure a little junk food, but the more we eat of it, the unhealthier we'll become.

The same is true with anything that comes from the soul. The soul cannot feed itself. And if our souls are being fed from the flesh, there may be moments of satisfaction, but we'll continue to become more needy of nourishment. This is not only blatant sins, but also religious practices, acts of human kindness, and other seemingly good things.

It's not wrong to look for opportunities to show kindness, nor is it wrong to participate in religious activities. But are these things acts of the flesh with the intent of feeding our need for a positive self-identity, or are they coming from a life filled with the Spirit that is now overflowing to the people around us?

If good deeds are our attempt to receive acceptance or self-identity, it is the empty works of the flesh. If it is the outward move from our spiritual life, it is the overflow of God's life of the Spirit. Are your works intake, our outflow? This helps to identify our spiritual condition. Are you trying to fulfill your needs, or are you giving out of a satisfied soul?

Religion cannot satisfy. Nor can it make us accepted by God. Do you know why your religious efforts can't make God accept you? Because God has already declared His acceptance of you through Christ. If you try to use religion to gain acceptance, it is a rejection of God's work for you, and substituting it with your work for Him. It is to snub God and say, "I can do better."

Sin can't satisfy. Religion can't satisfy. Charitable deeds can't satisfy. You are incomplete by design, because God has designed you to become one with Him. You were designed for intimacy with God. Look at **1 Corinthians 6:17**

But he who is joined to the Lord is one spirit *with Him*.

You are the glove; God is the hand that fills that glove. Without the hand, a glove is a lifeless object. Yet every human illustration falls short.

One illustration the Bible often uses is marriage. When a marriage is healthy and flourishing, the husband and wife are connected on every level. Their lives become so intertwined that neither can act without the other, and as they become one in mind, soul, and body, it becomes difficult to see where one ends and the other begins.

A bad marriage is when two people remain independent of one another. They don't think alike, are pulling in opposite directions, and there is little real unity. Instead of being intertwined, it becomes difficult to see where they are connected.

Many Christians live this way in their spiritual lives. God is inviting them into a spiritual life that will flow out to their soul and life in the physical world, but because they are focused on their physical world, intimacy never develops. Then they become a physical being trying to interact with the Spirit. This is where most Christians live. They try to find ways to visit God, instead of learning how to live in the life of intimate agape love God has ordained for them. They are living as if they are estranged, but have visitation rights.

The ONLY reason a Christian does not thrive is because they are stuck in the mindset of the flesh. They are trying to serve God through human effort instead of learning how to abide in the love of God in the Spirit.

You can't overcome because you are already an overcomer. The flesh can't mimic the life of the Spirit. Human effort produces a cheap substitute, but it only looks authentic to those who are not experiencing the real thing. Let's look at a few passages that affirm this. First look at **Romans 8:37**

> Yet in all these things we are more than conquerors through Him who loved us.

Are you more than a conqueror in this life? Are your struggles defeated before you? Are addictions and destructive behaviors falling out of your life? The truth is, you are already a conqueror – no, more than a conqueror – but this cannot be a reality in your life until you learn to walk in the Spirit. Look at this amazing promise in **1 John 5:4**

> For whatever is born of God overcomes the world. And this is the victory that has overcome the world-- our faith.

In this passage lies both our promise and the problem. The promise is that if you are born of God, you are already an overcomer. This is our new birth in Christ. The Bible does not tell us that we must be converted to Christianity. That is a mental decision to follow a religious system. You can remain unchanged inwardly while following religious believes outwardly.

Jesus explained this in John chapter 3. "Unless a man is born from above, he cannot see the Kingdom of God." Of course, this is referring to man in the general sense, such as mankind. This passage is often translated as born again, but when we look at the Greek word behind the translation, it becomes clearer. John 3:3 uses the term 'born again', which is 'gennao anothen' in the Greek. It means litteraly, born anew from above (or heaven). Let's add **2 Corinthians 5:17** to our discussion:

> Therefore, if anyone *is* in Christ, *he is* a new creation; old things have passed away; behold, all things have become new.

The Bible also refers to this event as 'the circumcision made without hands.' In the Old Testament ordinance of circumcision, a male child had the flesh of his foreskin cut away so he could enter into God's covenant of promise. This was a foreshadow of true circumcision. Colossians chapter 2 explains that our old nature of flesh was cut away by the Spirit, crucified with Christ, and buried. We are raised (or born again) with a new nature that is born of God.

This is when we hear about the promise of life in Christ, confess Him as Lord, and put our trust in Christ. When God invites us into His life, if we receive Him by faith, we are circumcised by the Spirit. Our old nature is taken away so we can enter into God's covenant of promise by faith. Then we are given a new spirit (which also gives us a new nature), and that is when all things become new.

Everything you have done in the flesh becomes old and passed away. Everything of God is new and is of the life of promise. The Old Testament law prepared the way for man to understand that righteousness cannot be produced by human effort, but the promise we now have was also foretold in the midst of the era of the law. Look at **Ezekiel 36:26-27**

> [26] "I will give you a new heart and put a new spirit within you; I will take the heart of stone out of your flesh and give you a heart of flesh.
> [27] "I will put My Spirit within you and cause you to walk in My statutes, and you will keep My judgments and do *them*.

We are now in that promise. When we trust in Him, God takes out our old nature and corrupted heart of sin, and places within us a new spirit that cannot be corrupted by sin.[5] Not only that, but He also places His Spirit within us. This is where true intimacy is born. Your new spirit and the Holy Spirit are in perfect fellowship, and as you learn to walk in that fellowship, your outward life will begin to reflect your inward life.

In the New Covenant, God does not command us to keep His ways by human effort. He says, "I will cause you to walk in my statutes." If you learn to walk according to your inward life, you will do by nature the things that please God. This is explained in **Romans 2:14-15a**

> [14] for when Gentiles, who do not have the law, by nature do the things in the law, these, although not having the law, are a law to themselves,
> [15] who show the work of the law written in their hearts,

When you are walking according to your new nature, you will do by nature the things that are right with God. You don't have to

---

[5] 1 Peter 1:23, 1 John 3:9

force yourself to do good. Nor do you have to force yourself to stop doing what is wrong. Look at this amazing promise in **Micah 7:19**

He will again have compassion on us, And will subdue our iniquities. You will cast all our sins Into the depths of the sea.

This was the coming promise given to the Old Testament people. We are now in that promise! Not only does God promise to forgive, but He also will subdue your iniquities. The word 'iniquity' means: perversion and depravity, wicked deeds, and acts of unrighteousness. A perversion is when something good is corrupted. Your emotions are easily perverted by the flesh. Destructive behavior is when iniquity is ruling our lives.

Our promise is that we are given a new nature. Our old nature is taken out of the way and crucified. We are given a new heart, new spirit, and we are given the gift of the Holy Spirit living within us. God takes all our sins and casts them into the sea of forgiveness. Not only were they cast in, but sent to the depths where they can never again emerge. Then the Lord promises to suppress our iniquities so they cannot overtake our lives. Finally, He promises that His Spirit working through our new spirit will cause us to naturally desire and do the things that are right.

To these things I ask, What is required of you? What is dependent upon you? If you are not experiencing these things, what is the reason? To find the answer, let's go back and look at our passage from **1 John 5:4**

For whatever is born of God overcomes the world. And this is the victory that has overcome the world-- our faith.

Whatever is born of God overcomes the world. Our new spirit is born of God, which means we are born of God. Our flesh is of the world. Sin is of the world. Life altering issues are of the world. So why do we struggle with these things? It is because religion teaches us to work, but God teaches us to rest in faith.

This is the victory that overcomes the world – our faith. Are you walking, living, and receiving by faith? Faith is in the finished work of Christ. Faith is in this promise found in **2 Peter 1:3-4**

³ His divine power has given to us all things that *pertain* to life and godliness, through the knowledge of Him who called us by glory and virtue,
⁴ by which have been given to us exceedingly great and precious promises, that through these you may be partakers of the divine nature, having escaped the corruption *that is* in the world through lust.

If God's power has given us all things that pertain to life and godliness, what do we lack? If all these amazing promises are given to us so we could become partakers of God's divine nature, then how to we live as overcomers?

It's all about faith. If I don't believe God has given me His righteousness, I will try to make myself righteous. If I don't believe I am holy in Christ, I'll try to become holy. If I don't believe I have escaped the corruption of the world, I'll battle the world through my own power.

Then I have faith in myself, faith in religion, or faith in what promises to gratify my flesh, but I don't have faith in Christ. If I don't have faith in the promise that I am an overcomer, I'll try to become an overcomer. If I don't believe that God can suppress my sinful weaknesses, I will turn to will power. When that fails, I'll trust in guilt, condemnation, and failure.

But you are victorious. In Christ you have overcome. You are more than a conqueror. More than a conqueror. The intent is that you understand that what troubles you is not only defeated, but defeated to the point to where it has become irrelevant – not even worthy of your focus. It is already ashes under your feet, but you have to be in Christ and have to learn to walk by faith – trusting in the reality that what God said is true, and that He has the power to do what He has said. And believe that you are exactly what God has declared over you.

Sin calls you a sinner. Addiction calls you an addict. Your problems, society, and people attempt to place you under a label, but the one who walks by faith stands upon God's strength. We don't even have to fight the label-makers. They are irrelevant. Don't let them become a distraction.

God does not want you to fight your battles. He doesn't want you to overcome your sins, failures, weaknesses, or life-issues. He wants you to let Him be your overcomer. He wants you to live by faith, not by the sight of the flesh.

The victorious life is the one who learns to be a receiver of grace. It is the one who trusts in God's power to suppress our enemies – both internally and externally. It's the person who learns to be one spirit with God. It's all about intimacy with God. The person who learns how to walk by faith will come short in nothing!

Stop trying to overcome, and start learning to walk by faith. This is the victory that overcomes the world – your faith! Have faith in Christ, what He has done, and what He has provided. Everything that pertains to this life has already been provided. Everything that we need to be godly has already been provided. Walk by faith and you can't be defeated. Live in this promise found in **Galatians 5:16**

I say then: Walk in the Spirit, and you shall not fulfill the lust of the flesh.

The flesh has no power over the person walking in faith. This is a promise. As you learn to walk in intimacy with God, you don't have to fight your life-controlling problems. They can't be fulfilled, for the life of the Spirit has rendered them powerless. But this promise cannot be received through anything other than learning how to walk in the intimacy of the Spirit.

Discussion Questions

Think about temptation. Why does some temptations appeal to one person, but have no drawing on another?

How do we overcome temptation? Does telling someone to resist, or warning them of judgment overcome temptation?

Read Hebrews 11:6. What does it take to please God?

Think about religious practices. How many of the things we've been taught mentioned in this passage?

How do we know the difference between the good works of the flesh, and good works through the Spirit?

Review Ezekiel 36:26-27. How does this apply to your Christian life? Can the Christian life be lived without receiving the promise of this passage?

Review Romans 2:14-15. Explain what it means to do by nature the things written in the law.

Read Romans 10:3, Romans 5:17, and Romans 4:6. Is the Bible telling us that grace gives us the power to keep the law, or is it that if we walk in the Spirit, it's in our nature to walk in agreement with God?

Read Romans 7:5 and Micah 7:19. How is sin defeated in our lives? What is our role?

If sin is hindering our life, what is the cause? What is the solution?

Review 1 John 5:4. What does this passage tell us about living the Christian life?

Review 2 Peter 1:3-4. What is not included in the phrase, "All things that pertain to life and godliness?" What does this teach you about walking by faith?

Review Galatians 5:16. How do we defeat the lusts of the flesh?

Is the Christian life about what we do for God, or what God has done for us through Christ? Explain.

True Faith

If faith is the victory that overcomes the world, then it is important to understand what faith is. Faith is not making yourself believe. Mark Twain once said, "Faith is believing something you know isn't true." Twain was observing religious superstition, but this isn't faith. Biblical faith is not man's attempt to force himself to believe. It's the heart responding to what God is revealing.

The church hasn't helped clarify the Bible's teaching on faith. Many are led to believe that we have to muster up faith in order to make God act. You may have heard statements like, "Faith activates God, but fear and doubt activates the devil."

False.

Do we really think God is a pushbutton genie that will come out of the Bible if we rub it the right way? You cannot activate God, nor can your faith or actions put God or angels in subjection to you. Sharing a Facebook post or typing 'Amen' will not grant you a wish from God. Nor is God displeased when you don't forward a picture of the 'Guilt trip Jesus' that demands you to share a picture or be declared as someone who is ashamed of Christ.

The reason people are so easily tossed by these winds of false doctrine is because they have no firm foundation. God is not a manipulator, nor is He manipulated by man. Faith is not a tool we use, or a force we tap into in order to gain god-like powers.

Faith is the revelation of God to us, with the invitation to put our trust in Him. God unveils His intention, gives us the power to receive and believe, then invites us to submit. Faith doesn't activate God. Faith activates you to enter into the work of the Spirit.

The word of God tells us what God intends for us, when we hear the word, the Spirit reveals truth to us, and then we are given the invitation to believe. The Bible says that faith comes by hearing the word of God.[6] Faith is a gift of the Spirit.[7] Romans 12:3 also affirms this by saying that God has dealt every person a measure of faith.

Making yourself believe is no better than trusting in a rabbit's foot, and you can see how much good that did for the rabbit!

Even so, people will boast about their faith and condemn others for a lack of faith. The truth is, you cannot produce faith. Not once in the Bible do we see the command to make ourselves believe or to produce faith. In fact, the same passage that tells us God deals each of us a measure of faith also warns us not to think that this is of ourselves.

The truth is, we build our lives upon faith. We do not build faith. When Jesus' disciples said, "Lord increase our faith," what did Jesus say? He made it clear that they already had sufficient faith. Then He used the illustration of a mustard seed. It was the smallest seed each person worked with. This small seed used for spice looks insignificant, but it illustrates the sufficiency of what God has provided. When we operate in God's gift of faith, nothing is impossible.

To illustrate further, Jesus pointed to the mulberry tree and the mountains. A mulberry tree is known for its deep roots and strong trunks. No one can pull up a mulberry tree by its roots. Yet Jesus said that the one acting in faith can tell it to be pulled up by the roots and cast into the sea, and it has to obey.

Then Jesus upped the ante. Look at the mountain. It is even more absurd to think we can move a mountain, yet the same power to pluck up the mulberry tree also renders the mountains powerless to stand. He said we could speak to the mountain and cast it into the sea.[8] Yet none of the promises of God are possible to us until we learn to walk in faith. Look at **Jude 1:20-21**

> [20] But you, beloved, building yourselves up on your most holy faith, praying in the Holy Spirit,

---

[6] Romans 10:17
[7] 1 Corinthians 12:9
[8] Luke 7:5-6, Matthew 21:21-22

^{21} keep yourselves in the love of God, looking for the mercy of our Lord Jesus Christ unto eternal life.

Somehow we have turned this powerful truth into an act of the human will. We've taken passages that teach us how to live by faith, and made them into man-dependent acts of the flesh. If you are like me, you've been taught this passage tells you to build up your faith. Read it again.

Build yourselves upon your most holy faith. Nothing you can produce can ever be called 'most holy'. There is only one source of holiness; our Most Holy God. And He has dealt us a measure of His most holy faith with the invitation to build our lives upon His foundation.

How many times did Jesus say, "How is it that you have no faith?" Why did He make these statements? Because He had revealed His power, yet people fell short of God's best because they chose to believe in the impossibility of the flesh, instead of the possibility that only comes by the Spirit.

Let's use an example. When the disciples of Jesus were caught in a storm on the Sea of Galilee, Jesus came to them walking on the water. At first, they were afraid and cried out, but Jesus called to them to not be afraid, "It is I." God revealed to Peter that if Christ was above the stormy waters, he knew that if He was with Christ, he also would be above the storms. In a moment of the revelation of faith, Peter stepped into the life of the Spirit. Look at **Matthew 14:28-31**

^{28} And Peter answered Him and said, "Lord, if it is You, command me to come to You on the water."

^{29} So He said, "Come." And when Peter had come down out of the boat, he walked on the water to go to Jesus.

^{30} But when he saw that the wind *was* boisterous, he was afraid; and beginning to sink he cried out, saying, "Lord, save me!"

^{31} And immediately Jesus stretched out *His* hand and caught him, and said to him, "O you of little faith, why did you doubt?"

Why did Peter have little faith? Did he need to do more to muster up greater faith? No. He did something no mortal man could do – he walked on the water. God revealed His intent to perform the miraculous in Peter's life. The word of God revealed God's purpose with the invitation, "Come." Faith comes by hearing the word of God.[9] Peter believed the word of Jesus and stepped out.

For a few precious steps, the water under Peter's feet became a firm foundation. The storm had no power because the waves of this world cannot touch the life in the Spirit. His eyes were on Christ and he was doing the impossible. Then he took his eyes out of faith and put them back into the world of human limitations, then all power disappeared.

"O you of little faith. Why did you doubt?" Jesus asked. Why did Peter let go of faith and receive the works of the flesh? The problem was not that Peter lacked faith. The problem was that Peter believed the waves over the invitation of faith. The waves could not overtake Peter; they could only beckon him to return to the flesh.

The same is true in your life and mine. God reveals to us the power of the Spirit, gives us the ability to believe, and then says, "Come. Come with Me in the Spirit. Let Me take you above the cares of this life. Let Me show you that problems have no power."

Sometimes we are like Peter. We take a few precious steps of faith and see the miraculous, but then we believe in doubt. We take our eyes off Christ, and begin focusing on the cares of this life again. We begin complaining, murmuring, or trust in disappointment. We forget to be receivers of joy, grace, and the abundant promises of God. The mind in the flesh loses the power of the Spirit. Then we become those of little faith. It isn't that faith is not present. It's that faith can't operate in the flesh.

Other times we are like the rest of the disciples. We sit in the boat and never want to leave the safety of what we know. The storm tossed boat that is taking on water is safer than stepping out

---

[9] Romans 10:17

The Best Advice I've Never Heard

into the storm, so we cling to the boat and try to paddle through trouble as best as we can. Our only hope is that God enters the boat and stops the storm, never comprehending that God wants to empower us to walk peacefully through the storm. God would rather teach you how to walk on the waves than trust in the safety of the boat.

Faith comes by revelation of the Spirit; not by human effort. Peter could have walked to the end of a peer and made himself believe that he could walk on water. Yet no matter how much he believed, if he stepped off the peer, he would splash. All the human faith he can muster cannot empower him to do the impossible.

I had a pastor friend who answered the call to preach. He felt God's call to leave his career behind and step out in faith. He did so and God supplied every need. Doors of opportunity opened and he said, "There wasn't a time when I wasn't preaching or ministering somewhere." He left his career and never looked back.

That was God's call for him to come. But many years later, I was in a class with several other young men called into ministry. He told this story and encouraged each one of us to follow that same path. He said, "God wants you to leave your careers, go to seminary, and God will provide through the ministry." He put a lot of pressure on us to follow the same path he followed.

Some of the men chose to quit their jobs and step out based on his leading. Others of us did not. After much prayer, God revealed to me in an unmistakable way that I was where He wanted me to be. In spite of what I felt God was telling me, this pastor pressured me to 'step out in faith'. But was it faith to step out without the Lord's call? As our mentor continued to press, another man in our group also quit work to devote to fulltime ministry.

Over the course of several months, the men who quit fell into hard times and financial distress. One even ended up in divorce. So why didn't God meet their needs as He did our mentor? It was not the call of faith. Not one of these men experienced the provision they expected. Some became disillusioned and left the ministry.

God never said, "Come," to me. Based on the results, it's clear God didn't call them to come either. God did call me to abandon my never-ending skill development in the Information Technology field. There came a day when God called me to trust Him, knowing that this fast changing field would leave me behind. God made it clear to me that I was to trust Him with my career, and He would use my employment to enable me to do ministry.

The miraculous happened time after time. I've written about this in other books, so I won't rehash it here. I will say that when the company was walking hundreds of people out, I was walking in. I got promotions when I thought I would get let go. I answered the call to stay, and God showed me His power to make a way where there was no way.

Faith is of the Spirit. If you are in Christ, you're a spiritual person. The Spirit reveals God's will to you, and God secures you with the promise and a call of faith. Then everything in the flesh will challenge you. Circumstances will prove that you cannot do what God has called you to do. This is by design. God doesn't want you to do the miraculous. God wants to do the miraculous in you. It's not possible to see God's power until it invites us to go beyond what we have the power to do ourselves. It isn't until this world becomes impossible that the power of the Spirit makes all things possible.

Most Christians never experience the power of God because they are only willing to go where the flesh can still have control. Yet equally important is that if we step into the impossible without the call of God, we are destined for failure and frustration.

Scripture gives a great example. Psalm 91 gives an amazing promise of God's protection and provision to those who learn to abide in His love. When Jesus was being tempted by Satan, the devil quoted from Psalm 91. "If you are the Son of God, cast yourself off this Temple, for it is written, 'He shall give His angels charge over you, to keep you, lest you dash your foot against a stone.'"

It's a promise of God, right? But Jesus refuted Satan by saying, "You shall not tempt the Lord your God." The word translated as 'tempt' literally means, 'to put God to the test'. Man flinging himself into harm's way and claiming it's an act of faith is false. Quitting your job without the call of the Spirit is putting God to the test. God is not obligated to save us from foolish choices. Yet when God calls a man to leave his career by stepping out in faith, that is God putting *us* to the test. And when God puts us to the test it is because He is planning to reveal His power to us – if we are willing to trust Him.

Knowing these things brings up the natural question. "How do I know when God is calling me to step out in faith." The truth is, most Christians are not capable of hearing God's voice, because they aren't listening. Faith comes by hearing the word of God, but if we are not seeking to know Him, we won't have the foundation to understand the difference between God's call, the ideas of other people, and random thoughts that pop into our heads. How do we know it isn't Satan saying, "If you are a child of God, prove your faith," thus putting the Lord to the test?

It's a question that can't be answered with formulas or theology. That answer can only come to those who learn how to hear God's voice. That comes through knowing Him – not knowing about Him.

The Christian life is not about doing our Christian duty. God is not pleased by what we do for Him. Reading your Bible does not please God. Going to church does not please Him. Giving money to church and doing good works does not please Him. A life that is pleasing God will produce all these things, but these things cannot produce a life that pleases God. Look at **Hebrews 11:6**

> But without faith *it is* impossible to please *Him*, for he who
> comes to God must believe that He is, and *that* He is a
> rewarder of those who diligently seek Him.

Jesus said that on the last day, many will say to Him, "We have fed the poor, done miracles, cast out demons, and done many mighty works in Jesus name," but He will say, "Depart from Me, I never knew you."

Serving in Jesus' name doesn't please God? Doing the very works Jesus said His followers would do doesn't please God? No. Without faith, it is impossible to please God. God reveals Himself to us, invites us into the life of the Spirit, and when we respond and receive, that pleases God. Then the Christian life is about diligently seeking God – not doing religious things.

God reveals Himself and His promises to us because He wants you to believe He is good, and that He wants you to receive His gifts of love. God wants you to believe Him. Receiving is an act of trust. The Spirit gives us the gift of faith, which is the power to see the purposes of God with the invitation to receive.

Then God also produces the fruit of the Spirit in us, who begin learning to abide in the Spirit. Part of the fruit of the Spirit is also faith. As we become receivers of what is revealed through faith, God begins to increase our capacity to see the greater things of faith, and become receivers of the deeper things of God. When we see a great man or woman of faith, they don't have a special anointing of God. They have learned to believe in what God is revealing, and as they receive, they grow in their ability to receive all the more.

Jesus also explained this when He said, "To the one who has (possesses), more will be given, and he will have in abundance. The one who doesn't have, even that which he has will be taken away."[10] You have the gift of faith. As you receive the revelation of faith, more will be given, and you will overflow with abundance. If you neglect faith, you will lack.

Faith is the gift of the Spirit, which you have been given. God desires to produce the abundant fruit through the faith He has placed in you, and then produce the fruit of the Spirit through your abundance of faith. Don't be the one Jesus says, "O you of little faith. Why did you doubt?"

Let's conclude this chapter with **Hebrews 11:1**

Now faith is the substance of things hoped for, the evidence of things not seen.

Human eyes can't see what has been revealed to the eyes of faith. Faith is the substance (or evidence) of our hope. Hope isn't merely the way we normally define it. We say, "I hope so," when we want something to turn out well. That is not biblical hope. Hope

---

[10] Matthew 13:12, Matthew 25:29, Mark 4:25, Luke 8:18

The Best Advice I've Never Heard

is the confident expectation of what God has promised. His word is certain, so we have confidence in what God has given us hope to receive. Then we have all the evidence we need to operate in our spiritual walk of faith.

Walking in faith is walking in the Spirit. We believe what God has revealed, and we walk according to the spiritual life of promise, regardless of what the physical world presents against hope. Faith overcomes the world, both in our outward life, and our inner struggles of the flesh. Our weaknesses are defeated when we become receivers of God's power through faith.

The person who abides in faith has opened the channels of the life of the Spirit to flow into their lives in this world. Then the power of the Spirit takes the hope of God's promise and reveals to us how to receive them. That is the person who will come short of no gift.

Faith overcomes, because faith receives the unstoppable purposes of God. Then nothing is impossible!

Discussion Questions

What is the source of faith?

Did God give us faith to use as something to force Him to act?

Read Jude 1:20-21. Explain what the Bible means by, "Build yourselves upon your most holy faith."

What makes faith 'most holy'?

Review Matthew 14:28-31. What caused Peter to walk on the water?

What caused Peter to start operating in the flesh again?

Was Peter lacking in faith when He stepped out?

Did Peter not have enough faith to finish his walk to Jesus?

When is it an act of faith to put God to the test?

How do we discern between our emotions, human thoughts, and the prompting of the Spirit?

Read Matthew 25:29. How does this apply to our faith?

Read Hebrews 11:1. Explain the definition of faith.

Explain what 'hope' means to the Christian.

Why is it impossible to please God without faith?

Has your perspective on faith changed? If so, in what way?

Resting in Acceptance

Human acceptance is conditional, and because we have been conditioned to think on the level of human nature, we impose that view into our relationship with God. With people, we can hide our shortcomings, but we know God sees every action and attitude, whether good or bad. For this reason, if our understanding of acceptance is flawed, our faith will be undermined by our own sense of self-worth. When we've done enough things right, we'll feel accepted. When we mess up or fail to perform, we'll feel rejected.

This view of God is flawed to the point of disaster. It's one of the main reasons Christians live under feelings of fear and condemnation. It is also the reason spiritual maturity is suppressed. Until I feel accepted by God, my growth will be crippled.

Part of the reason Christians are trapped in the performance mindset is because of the misapplication of the Old Testament. The Bible says the law is good IF it is used legitimately. If it isn't properly applied, then it becomes corrupt. Look at **1 Timothy 1:8-9b:**

> 8 But we know that the law is good if one uses it lawfully,
> 9 knowing this: that the law is not made for a righteous person, but for the lawless and insubordinate, for the ungodly and for sinners,

According to the Bible, we are the righteousness of God in Christ. When we have faith, we are imputed with God's righteousness. God accounts us as righteous, but the law is not for the righteous person. So why are we putting ourselves under a condemnation system that was not intended for the saints?

The word 'lawfully' in the above passage means: legitimately or properly. The truth is that the law is designed with three main purposes. **One:** It was given because of transgressions.[11] It was intended to keep people in check until Christ came. **Two:** It was

---

[11] Galatians 3:19

given to reveal to mankind that we are sinners that cannot rise to the level of true righteousness. God gave the law to unveil man's guilt.[12] **Three**: The law was given to point us to Christ. Look at **Galatians 3:22-25**

> [22] But the Scripture has confined all under sin, that the promise by faith in Jesus Christ might be given to those who believe.
> [23] But before faith came, we were kept under guard by the law, kept for the faith which would afterward be revealed.
> [24] Therefore the law was our tutor to bring us to Christ, that we might be justified by faith.
> [25] But after faith has come, we are no longer under a tutor.

We are no longer under a tutor? When we entered faith, we graduated out of the law and into grace. This goes back to 1 Timothy. The law is not given for the righteous man, but for the ungodly and the sinner. Once we are under righteousness, we are no longer under the tutelage of the law. The reason is that once we have the Spirit within us, the external world of the law becomes irrelevant in God's eyes. We are guided by the internal leading of the Spirit. The New Testament is filled with the teaching that we are not under the law for a reason. First, let's look at a few passages that affirm this:

Romans 6:14

> For sin shall not have dominion over you, for you are not under law but under grace.

Galatians 4:4-5

> [4] But when the fullness of the time had come, God sent forth His Son, born of a woman, born under the law,
> [5] to redeem those who were under the law, that we might receive the adoption as sons.

Romans 10:4

---

[12] Romans 3:19-20

For Christ is the end of the law for righteousness to everyone who believes.

Galatians 5:18

But if you are led by the Spirit, you are not under the law.

There is a reason why the Bible teaches these things. Your righteousness is not your gift to God, but His gift to you. The Bible says that Jesus became sin for you, that you might become the righteousness of God in Him.[13]

If you don't understand this one basic truth, you'll always feel inadequate in your relationship with God. The law was designed to show you that righteousness comes from God alone and not from man. Grace reveals that you are righteous because God has gifted you with His righteousness, and that sin is now rendered powerless – even to the point of irrelevance.

God does not want you to look at your sins, but at His gift of righteousness invested in you. The Old Testament's command was, "Look at yourself. Because sin remains, you are not worthy to come before Me." Instead of instructing us to look at our attempts to be good against the law, the New Covenant commands us to look at Christ. Under the New Covenant, God never tells us to look at ourselves. "Look to Christ," is the focus of the New Testament.

The fall of man began when he declared that he could be good without God. The law was given to man because he still believed he could be like God. "We will do all that is in the law," the people declared when the law was given. The law is not a merit system; it is a condemnation system. It never rewards for doing good; it condemns when we fall short.

The great irony is that the blessing of God has always been outside the law. When man came under the law, any who fell short of righteousness were placed under the curse of the law, where the blessing was out of reach. Since the Bible says that all have sinned and fallen short of the glory of God, not one person under the law qualified for the abundant blessing of God.

---

[13] 2 Corinthians 5:21

Resting in Acceptance

Before the law came, God's people were blessed for their faith – not for their righteous acts. It was not until the law came that God's favor was based on man's worthiness. Then after Christ redeemed us from the law, we are again under the blessing of faith, not the perfect demands of the law.

Adam did nothing to earn the paradise of God. Eden was a gift without merit. It was when Adam stepped out of faith and tried to become his own source of goodness that the curse began. The era of the law was intended to drive man's self-righteousness to despair so he could again see that righteousness comes from God alone.

When the fullness of time had come, God sent His son to fulfill the law, and become a curse for us. The fullness of time was when the law finished its work of unveiling sin. Once that was accomplished, the Bible says, "But now, once at the end of the ages, He has appeared to put away sin by the sacrifice of Himself."[14]

The New Testament is all about God's love toward you. Sin has been defeated so you can come before Him without fear or condemnation. Look at **Romans 5:8-10**

[8] But God demonstrates His own love toward us, in that while we were still sinners, Christ died for us.

[9] Much more then, having now been justified by His blood, we shall be saved from wrath through Him.

[10] For if when we were enemies we were reconciled to God through the death of His Son, much more, having been reconciled, we shall be saved by His life.

Notice that this is not only talking about your salvation, but the continuous life of the Christian. If God demonstrated His love toward you while you were a sinner, how much more does His love work in your life now that you are a child of God?

You have been saved from wrath through Christ. Now God commands you to walk by a new law – the law of faith.[15] The Law of the New Covenant is faith in what Christ has accomplished, not

---

[14] Hebrews 9:26
[15] Romans 3:26-28

Resting in Acceptance

what you can do for Him. The law of faith is about trusting in the power of God's love, not the power of sin. The New Covenant is about your acceptance, not your condemnation. Meditate on this wonderful passage in **Ephesians 1:6**

> To the praise of the glory of His grace, by which He made us accepted in the Beloved.

Do you know why you are accepted by God? You are accepted in the Beloved. You are accepted because you are in Christ. It has nothing to do with sin. It has nothing to do with what you do or don't do. You are acceptable to God because your sin was judged in Christ, and you trusted in Christ. Because of this, you are now the righteousness of God in Christ. Is there any more righteous than God? If there is no higher righteousness, there is nothing lacking. Any attempt at righteousness is now a step down.

Is your sin greater than God's power? Can your sin defeat the work of Christ? Can sin defeat God's righteousness? Absolutely not. If it could, then man's work is more powerful than God's. Anyone who believes their sins take them out of God's favor is declaring that they believe man has more power than God.

Remember, the Bible compares the work of Adam to the work of Christ. Without any work on our part, we are born into Adam's sin. We inherited our sin nature from Adam, and even when we try to work our way into righteousness, we find ourselves in the prison of sin. A sinner who does good is still a sinner. A person with a sinful nature doesn't change their nature by doing an act of kindness.

In the same way, the Bible says that Jesus much more overcame the work of Adam. In Adam all die, even so in Christ are all made alive.[16] Then to show us the power of grace over sin, the Bible says that where sin abounded, grace much more abounded over sin.[17] Sin cannot stand in the presence of grace. Satan knows this, so to keep us from super-abounding over sin, he persuades us that sin nullifies grace. Then we waste our lives trying to drive out

---

[16] 1 Corinthians 15:22
[17] Romans 5:20

sin by personal righteousness, not understanding that the only people who abound over sin are those who abound in grace.

If you doubt the power of grace, you will be defeated by sin. If you limit grace, you limit your victory over sin. If you doubt God's love, your heart becomes the source of condemnation – not God. According to the Bible, the one who knows and believes in the love of God is the one who is perfected.[18] Not only this, but according to 1 John 4:16, the person who abides in God's love abides in God. Our command is to know and believe in the love He has for us.

Do you want to draw closer to God? Believe in God's love for you. Abide in His love and let His love transform you into His image. It's the simplicity of the gospel that unveils the power of God to us. But we complicate it by taking our eyes off grace and putting them onto ourselves. We have no understanding of how to make our lives conform to God's image, and we're not supposed to. That's God's job. Our job is to see the promise of God's love and believe. Our job is to see the promise of unearnable grace, and believe it.

People don't believe because they are so caught up into a focus on sin that they lose sight of God's complete acceptance, and then they stop believing in His love and grace. The fear of sin can be put to rest in a single passage. Look at **Romans 4:3-8**

3 For what does the Scripture say? " Abraham believed God, and it was accounted to him for righteousness."

4 Now to him who works, the wages are not counted as grace but as debt.

5 But to him who does not work but believes on Him who justifies the ungodly, his faith is accounted for righteousness,

6 just as David also describes the blessedness of the man to whom God imputes righteousness apart from works:

7 " Blessed are those whose lawless deeds are forgiven, And whose sins are covered;

8 Blessed is the man to whom the Lord shall not impute sin."

---

[18] 1 John 4:12, 17-18

Resting in Acceptance

The first thing to note is that righteousness is a gift received by faith. Grace becomes unattainable the moment we make it about what we do for God instead of trusting in what He has done for us. The moment our work comes into focus, grace is out of focus. That's why the average Christian does not experience the power of grace.

Next, take note of the three-fold blessing given to those who believe God. You are blessed because your sins are forgiven. That is your past. Everything is taken out of the way because it was paid through Christ. Once you believe, you receive this promise. That's the first blessing.

Second, you are blessed because God imputes righteousness to you. Without works or human effort, you are blessed because God imputes His righteousness to you. God credits you as though you are as righteous as Himself! Let that sink in for a moment. Look at the perfect righteousness of God. None is higher. Nothing more can be accomplished. That same righteousness is credited to you by God. God declares you as His child, and God says, "You are my righteousness." This is why you are accepted. You are God's righteousness and it is a gift of His love. All God asks is that you trust in His gift of love.

Third, blessed is the one whom the Lord SHALL NOT impute sin. There is only one person's sin that could be imputed to you – that is the sins you actually commit. But because you are now delivered from the law, there is no law to condemn you. You are now blessed because God has promised that He shall not impute your sins to you.

Doesn't that make you want to sing, Amazing Grace?

This means you cannot lose your acceptance. Even when you sin, you are still accepted by God and blameless before Him. This is why 1 John 2:1 promises, "If anyone sins, we have an Advocate, Jesus Christ the righteous." An advocate is a legal defender that pleads the innocence of his client. If Jesus is your advocate, and all authority has been given to Him, and He is the perfection of righteousness, if He declares you are innocent, you are innocent. And this is written as encouragement to us when we HAVE sinned.

Do you believe God? Do you believe He is your advocate? Do you believe the promise that God imputes righteousness and will not impute sin?

Once a Christian begins to believe this, and follows the command to abide in God's love, and obeys the promise that if we behold the glory of Christ, we are transformed into that same image, the transformation truly begins.

While faithless religion says, "This can't work. If you tell people that they can never again be under sin, this will cause people to sin more," the opposite is true. These are the ONLY people who truly overcome sin. It loses power because the Spirit flows freely, and since everything of God is received by faith, this is the only believer in a position to receive the fullness of grace.

Sin cannot defeat grace. Grace triumphs over sin. I did not experience victory over the sins that defeated me until I stopped trying to overcome, and began to rest in these promises. The altar of condemnation could not shame me enough to drive out sin. But grace changed my life.

When sharing this message of grace, I had a man confront me by saying, "You have secret sin in your life. You are just trying to justify your own sin." After his accusation, he couldn't point out any sins that he supposedly knew were in my life. I thought on the irony of this accusation.

When I was proclaiming the law, I had secret sins in my life. I tried in vain to overcome them, but they were too strong for me. Even when I was reading my Bible, my sins overtook me and dragged my mind back into corruption. The greater irony is that those who are hiding sin are often the ones who condemn others the most. Many of the most vocal critics against sin have been publicly shamed by being caught in the same sins they condemned. They are the first to hold up the law and proclaim the guilt of others. Think about the church scandals in the last few decades. How many were condemning people for their sins? The last three big name preachers that fell into scandal, were all secretly committing the very sins they were condemning. Yet this same legalistic shadow of Christianity accuses grace believers of living for sin.

Under the law, I could easily condemn others, but I could not fix myself. But under grace – the fullness of grace – my secret sins were overrun and driven out of my life. Now I don't have to keep them a secret, for they are trophies of grace. To personalize Romans 8:3, What I could not do under the law because of the weakness of my flesh, God accomplished by sending Christ, who condemned my sin in His own flesh, and fulfilled the righteous requirement of the law on my behalf, when I began to live according to the Spirit.

Stop worrying about sin. Stop focusing on yourself. You are not accepted because of anything other than faith in Christ. Defeating your sin is God's job. He has taken condemnation out of the way so you can know you are free to walk by faith in the Spirit. The only thing that can defeat you is trusting in doubt.

Rejoice in the work of Christ and the gift of grace, and as you walk in acceptance, watch God crush sin under your feet! It has no power, for you are no longer under the law, but under grace. The strength of sin is the law, but because you are no longer under that law, it has no strength. This is true for any who walk according to faith. Don't empower sin, walk by faith!

Discussion Questions

Review 1 Timothy 1:8-9. Who is the law written to?

Read Romans 5:17-19. Who is the righteous person?

Review Galatians 3:22-25. Who is the tutor?

When are we no longer under that tutor?

What did Adam have to do to earn the Garden of Eden (the paradise of God)?

Read Genesis 3:5. Did Adam and Eve know good before taking the fruit of temptation?

When Adam decided to become his own source of goodness, did he find good?

Read Genesis 15:1-6 and Romans 4:4-8. What did Abraham do to become righteous?

What does it take to be under the blessing of righteousness?

According to Romans 4:8, what judgment of sin comes to those who are under the blessing of faith?

Review Ephesians 1:6. Why are you accepted by God?

Can your sin defeat the work of Christ?

Does sin have more power than the righteousness of God?

What drives out sin, keeping the law, or trusting in grace?

Read Romans 5:13, Romans 6:15, Galatians 5:18, and read again Romans 4:8. Why are our sins not imputed?

Read Romans 6:14. Does believing in grace empower us to sin? Why or why not?

Read 1 Corinthians 15:56. What gives strength to sin?

Has your perspective on the law, and your acceptance by God changed? If so, explain.

Flesh Versus the Spirit

The frustrated Christian life occurs when we try to live for God instead of allowing Christ to live through us. If you try to live for God, you will fail. You might have limited success toward religion, but you will not discover the depth of what God has designed for you. Let's begin by looking at **Galatians 2:20**

> I have been crucified with Christ; it is no longer I who live, but Christ lives in me; and the life which I now live in the flesh I live by faith in the Son of God, who loved me and gave Himself for me.

You aren't supposed to live for God, but allow God to crucify your life of the flesh. If you go back and read the passages that precede verse 20, the Apostle Paul is explaining that the law put him under condemnation. He lived as perfect as he possibly could, but when he discovered Christ, his self-righteousness and religious works became trash in Paul's eyes.

The flesh cannot produce righteousness. Righteousness is a gift of the Spirit, and the life of righteousness is the life of the Spirit flowing through us. It is a life of faith, not of works. Faith does its work, but works cannot produce faith or the work of the Spirit.

The weaknesses of the flesh are nullified in the life of the Spirit. Most people try to live the Christian life by attempting to break the strongholds of the flesh by human effort. We tend to think, *If I can get this sin out of my life, I'll be right with God.*

Not so. It is the Spirit who gives life, and the Spirit that drives out the flesh. It is not we who make room for the Spirit, but the Spirit that drives out anything that hinders the life of the Spirit when we yield ourselves to Him. Look at **2 Corinthians 10:4**

> For the weapons of our warfare are not carnal but mighty in God for pulling down strongholds.

It is the might of the Spirit that pulls down strongholds. Our role is to yield to God through faith, and then allow the Spirit to do its work. It is not your job to fix yourself. God has established the life of faith to center upon Him, so that when you learn to walk by faith, your outward behavior will naturally conform to the inner life of the Spirit. Look at Micah 7:

> **18** Who *is* a God like You, Pardoning iniquity and passing over the transgression of the remnant of His heritage? He does not retain His anger forever, Because He delights *in* mercy.
> **19** He will again have compassion on us, and will subdue our iniquities. You will cast all our sins into the depths of the sea.

This is why it is vital to understand the life of the Spirit versus the life of the flesh. If you try to live the Christian life through the flesh, you are using a lifestyle that is incompatible with the Spirit in the hopes of uniting with the Spirit. It's not going to happen. The flesh and the Spirit will never have union. To understand this, look at **Romans 8:3-8**

> **3** For what the law could not do in that it was weak through the flesh, God *did* by sending His own Son in the likeness of sinful flesh, on account of sin: He condemned sin in the flesh,
> **4** that the righteous requirement of the law might be fulfilled in us who do not walk according to the flesh but according to the Spirit.
> **5** For those who live according to the flesh set their minds on the things of the flesh, but those *who live* according to the Spirit, the things of the Spirit.
> **6** For to be carnally minded *is* death, but to be spiritually minded *is* life and peace.
> **7** Because the carnal mind *is* enmity against God; for it is not subject to the law of God, nor indeed can be.
> **8** So then, those who are in the flesh cannot please God.

This passage begins with the explanation that what could not be accomplished because of the weakness of the flesh, Jesus accomplished for us. Sin was defeated in Jesus' flesh, that the righteous requirement of the law might be fulfilled in us who walk in the Spirit by faith.

If you are sinning in the flesh, you cannot please God. But the problem doesn't stop there. If you are serving Christ in your flesh, you still cannot please God. In your flesh, you can NEVER please God. Keeping the Ten Commandments doesn't change the flesh into the life of the Spirit. Doing works, avoiding temptation, reading the Bible, and going to church doesn't make human effort become a work of the Spirit.

It isn't works, but spiritual mindedness. We just read that those who are not in the Spirit cannot please God. Hebrews 11:6 explains that without faith it is impossible to please God. Faith and the Spirit are inseparable. Grace is the fullness of God's love given to us through the Spirit, and we receive by faith. Without faith, God's favor remains, but we don't believe, and therefore, can't receive.

Without faith it is impossible to please God because if you don't believe, you are rejecting the love of God. Everything is by grace through faith. God's grace (or favor toward you) is the expressions of God's love, and through faith (recognizing and trusting in the grace God is revealing) we receive. A distrusting Christian can never please God.

Grace remains unrealized when we either try to earn it through the flesh, or account ourselves as unworthy because we are measuring ourselves according to the flesh.

You *do not* have to get your flesh right with God. Let me reiterate this. You do not have to conform your flesh to a godly standard before you can receive grace. If you try, you are in the flesh, where grace becomes unattainable.

The problem is that most Christians do not comprehend the reality that the flesh and the Spirit are the antithesis of each other, and even at our best, the flesh is still the flesh and will always be at war with the Spirit. On the other hand, the flesh at its worst cannot nullify the grace of God. Once we enter the promise of faith, the flesh becomes irrelevant and powerless.

When we blow it and sin, grace is NOT withdrawn. We have become deceived into trusting in the flesh, and have stepped out of faith and into the carnal, or natural man. The solution is not to take the carnal mind and beat our flesh with guilt, remorse, and human repentance. I say human because there is a false repentance.

Judas repented and it destroyed him. Many people repent in the flesh, and they never find peace or rest for their souls. Suicide is often a form of repentance. Guilt, shame, and misery are forms of human repentance. Beating yourself with guilt does not produce godliness. This does NOT mean that Christians never sorrow over sin. Sorrow often produces true repentance.

When the Corinthian church had a member actively living a sinful lifestyle, the church was rebuked for welcoming it, and the person was given a choice to repent or be excluded from fellowship. In the end, he was very sorrowful over his sin, was welcomed back into fellowship, and the Bible affirms that godly sorrow produces repentance. In the same passage, the Bible also says that worldly sorrow leads to death.

We confuse repentance with sorrow. Repentance does not mean to sorrow over your sins or be wracked with guilt. Repentance means 'to change the mind'. It literally means to change the mind from the flesh to the Spirit. Godly sorrow is when we recognize the valuelessness of sin and we regret investing our lives in it. Often this occurs when we see what good looks like.

The Bible says, "The goodness of God leads you to repentance." Sin only looks good because we don't know what true good looks like. Once we begin discovering the treasures of our life in Christ, sin appears to be sin, instead of appearing to be good.

Godless sorrow is the regret we feel for our sins, life's choices, or our failures. We are not looking at God; we are looking at ourselves. There is nothing to change the mind to, so our mind remains in the flesh and is swallowed up with self-focused sorrow. The sorrow of the world does not see the grace of God, so this form of repentance leads toward death.

Unfortunately, the church often teaches a self-focused style of repentance. "Look at your sins. Look at your failures. Look at how much you fall short of God's commandments." This can only produce fleshly sorrow (which is what the world has), but it doesn't produce godly repentance, or a godly change of the mind. This is evident because in many churches, people are driven to the altar to sorrow and plead for mercy, but there is no long-term life change. There is only a temporary unloading of guilt.

When I look at my failures and faults, I lose hope. When I look at Christ, I see the goodness of God's grace, the worthlessness of my flesh, and the hope of life in the Spirit. I'm not beaten down with the guilt of the weakness of my flesh. I'm called out of the flesh and invited to exchange my weakness of the flesh for the strength of the Spirit.

This is why many people have been believers for decades, repent constantly, but never mature and never find victory. Worldly repentance cannot work. Preaching a repentance that directs people to look at their flesh cannot produce spiritual maturity. The flesh can only try to do better, but it cannot change. It also cannot have much success at trying to do better, either.

Let's take a few moments to look at the foundational principles of how we are translated from the flesh to the Spirit.

Spirit, Soul, and Body

Let's begin with **1 Thessalonians 5:23**
Now may the God of peace Himself sanctify you completely; and may your whole spirit, soul, and body be preserved blameless at the coming of our Lord Jesus Christ.

Many make the mistake of looking at the soul and the spirit as if they are the same thing. They are not. The soul is our will, personality, emotions, and the things that make us into individuals. The body is the physical part of us that interacts with the world. The spirit is the part of us that interacts with the life of the Spirit. It is the part of us that has been born again, where God also gave us a new nature.

Remember the passage we read from Ezekiel in a previous chapter? God promised that He would give us a new spirit *and* He would place His Spirit within us. From this fellowship in the Spirit, we have the promise that He will cause us to walk in His ways, and through our new spirit, we can have a life of obedience.

The life of the Spirit is to walk in the sanctified life. This also can be a point of confusion. If you are like me, you may have heard it taught that Jesus justifies you, but now you must work to become sanctified. This is false. Your new life is sanctified. It has to be, else you could not have a life that is hidden in Christ. Sin cannot survive in God's presence. The entire Old Testament drives this point home. The entire New Testament drives home the point that we have been set apart for God and are cleansed in Christ. That is what the word sanctified means – to be set apart for God. Look at these two passages:

> **1 Corinthians 6:11** And such were some of you. But you were washed, but you were sanctified, but you were justified in the name of the Lord Jesus and by the Spirit of our God.

> **Hebrews 10:10** By that will we have been sanctified through the offering of the body of Jesus Christ once for all.

Notice the past tense of these passages. You were washed. You were sanctified. You have been sanctified. Your sanctification is an accomplished fact. You are not trying to become set apart for God; you have been set apart for God by the Spirit who sanctified you.

Don't try to use 1 Thessalonians 5:23 against the rest of scripture, as some do. These passages complement each other. In the Spirit, you were sanctified. But your body is not. To help understand this, look at **Romans 8:10**

> And if Christ is in you, the body is dead because of sin, but the Spirit is life because of righteousness.

You are in Christ and your spirit is alive because of God's righteousness, but your body is still corrupted by sin. When the Bible tells us to be completely sanctified, spirit, soul, and body, it is a call to live according to the inward man, so your outward life can be aligned with your inward life. Complete sanctification is when your mind and body are walking in the life of the Spirit.

Complete sanctification has to come from the inside out. It can never work from the outside in. You can't make your body and mind conform to God's will without the power of the Spirit. Frustration and failure is the result of trying to use the fleshly mind to fulfill our spiritual calling.

God has sanctified you through the blood of Christ and the washing of the Spirit. You are now called to walk by faith so your mind is brought in line with the reality of what God has already accomplished through the Spirit. To help understand this, let's also look at **Romans 8:11**

But if the Spirit of Him who raised Jesus from the dead dwells in you, He who raised Christ from the dead will also give life to your mortal bodies through His Spirit who dwells in you.

The Spirit of God will give life to your mortal, or physical bodies, through the Spirit. This is the natural result of our mind being set on the Spirit. To clarify this further, I want to bring in three additional scriptures that explain this.

Romans 8:5 For those who live according to the flesh set their minds on the things of the flesh, but those who live according to the Spirit, the things of the Spirit.

Romans 7:25 I thank God—through Jesus Christ our Lord! So then, with the mind I myself serve the law of God, but with the flesh the law of sin.

Ephesians 4:
[22] that you put off, concerning your former conduct, the old

man which grows corrupt according to the deceitful lusts,
23 and be renewed in the spirit of your mind,
24 and that you put on the new man which was created according to God, in true righteousness and holiness.

Each of these passages is explaining the same principle. Your flesh serves sin. There is nothing you can do to change this fact. Even if you are trying to do good, you are still serving sin. Sinful flesh cannot produce righteousness, nor can it enter the life of the Spirit, or give aid to the life of the Spirit. You are called to put off the body of flesh. You are not called to reform it. Good works cannot emerge until the body is unemployed, and the mind is in line with the Spirit.

The mind set on the Spirit is in life. The mind set on the flesh is in death. If you take the time to study the books of Hebrews and Romans, you will see that the Bible calls those who are trying to do the works of the law a people whose minds are set on the flesh. The mind in the flesh is not only pursuing what we consider as blatant sins. The mind pursuing Christianity through human effort is just as much in the flesh as the mind on sin.

The mind set on sin is rebelling against God's promise of satisfaction, and trying to become gratified without God. The mind set on religion is rebelling against God's promise that He is our righteousness. The fleshly mind is trying to become righteous apart from God. These are merely two ends of the same spectrum of the flesh.

The mind set on the Spirit is the mind that believes God. Abraham was doing nothing religious when God declared him as righteous. Abraham longed for a son to carry on the family name. God promised that Abraham would have a son through his barren wife, Sarah. Abraham believed this promise, and God not only gave him the promised son, but credited Abraham with God's own righteousness for no other reason than that Abraham believed God.

God hasn't changed. When you believe that God has destroyed sin and given you His righteousness in its place, you are accounted as though you are the righteousness of God. When you believe God's promise of grace, you are credited with God's righteousness *and* the promises of grace.

Titus 2:11-14 promises you that grace (God's unearned favor toward you) brings you salvation, teaches you to deny ungodliness and lust, teaches you how to have a sober mind and live godly and righteously in the midst of a godless age, and it also creates in you a passion for good works.

Those who don't believe grace can really do what God has promised will fall back into the flesh to attempt to do it themselves. Those who believe God and trust in His grace will receive all these promises, will be pleasing to God simply because they believe Him, and He accounts them as perfectly righteous apart from any works or failure.

The sinner is accounted as righteous by faith, and then the righteousness of grace begins to transform that person into the image of Christ. And all we have to do is walk in the promise.

Most Christians don't believe grace is true. They are stuck in the flesh, which believes grace is merely a power source for the flesh.

God will never empower you to do what Jesus has already done. Those who try to obey God by becoming righteous for God, or sanctify themselves for God, are making themselves a rival of Jesus. God will not honor those who dishonor the Son. To count the blood of the New Covenant as a common thing does not impress God. Hebrews 10:29 warns us that to do so is to despise the Spirit of Grace.

To count the blood of the Covenant (which is Jesus' sacrifice) as a common thing is to put our common works on par with Jesus'. When I try to become righteous, I am putting my righteousness on par with God's, which makes the gift of righteousness that comes through grace a common thing. If we can accomplish righteousness, then Jesus' works are common to all.

Righteousness is a gift of grace, and it reigns when the flesh is unemployed. Let's look at **Romans 6:5-8**

> 5 For if we have been united together in the likeness of His death, certainly we also shall be in the likeness of His resurrection,
> 6 knowing this, that our old man was crucified with Him, that the body of sin might be done away with, that we should no longer be slaves of sin.
> 7 For he who has died has been freed from sin.
> 8 Now if we died with Christ, we believe that we shall also live with Him

You have been freed from sin. Period. Your body is still dead because of sin, but you are alive because of God's righteousness. The above passages can be confusing because of the way they are translated. Some translations say the body is destroyed. The NKJV above says, 'done away with'. The Bible isn't saying the body is destroyed, but unemployed. The Greek word translated into 'done away with' is the word 'katargeo', which means to be rendered useless or unemployed.

It's important to understand this, otherwise we can't understand why we sin. I want to bring in a passage that helps clarify this in a moment, but first let's review **Colossians 2:11-12**

> 11 In Him you were also circumcised with the circumcision made without hands, by putting off the body of the sins of the flesh, by the circumcision of Christ,
> 12 buried with Him in baptism, in which you also were raised with Him through faith in the working of God, who raised Him from the dead.

In this book, important principles are repeated because it's important to reiterate them. We are having contradictory messages taught in the name of Christianity that undermine faith. So we need to shore up these things so we learn to walk in scriptural truth.

In a previous chapter we talked about circumcision. This is where it becomes important. Your flesh nature and fleshly heart was taken away. It was cut out of you by the circumcision of God.

When this occurred, the body of flesh that once controlled our sinful nature became unemployed. Here is a passage that helps add to that explanation, **Hebrews 4:12**

> For the word of God is living and powerful, and sharper than any two-edged sword, piercing even to the division of soul and spirit, and of joints and marrow, and is a discerner of the thoughts and intents of the heart.

When the word of God is taught and someone receives the promise of salvation, their old nature is cut away, and the Spirit divides the soul from the spirit. There is a reason for this.

In our life before Christ, the spirit was dead to God.[19] Our dead spirit was unemployed. The soul ruled the dead spirit, and the body ruled the soul. When the body craved satisfaction, it demanded the mind serve its bidding and our minds looked for ways to gratify our cravings, both good and bad.

When the Spirit circumcised our old nature away, God also divided our soul from our spirit, gave us a new spirit, and now calls us to walk according to the Spirit of life, which is the Holy Spirit, who is always giving life to our new spirit. Or as **Galatians 5:25** states:

> If we live in the Spirit, let us also walk in the Spirit.

That 'if' can be misunderstood also. This is written to the church and is stating that if/since this is true (that you live in the Spirit), let us also walk in the Spirit. Romans 8:9 clearly states that any who are in Christ are in the Spirit. Yet if I am not walking in the Spirit, which is to walk by faith, I will be walking in the flesh. There is not a neutral position. You are either walking in the flesh, or walking in the Spirit.

Your mind is the battle ground between the flesh and the Spirit. The mind on the flesh produces death. The mind in the Spirit produces life.[20] You are either operating in faith, or in the flesh. When your mind is in the flesh, you are in sin. Your unemployed

---

[19] Ephesians 2:1, Ephesians 2:5
[20] Romans 8:5-6

flesh still craves sin, and if you starve your spirit, the flesh will appear strong. Let's look at this war as described in **Romans:7**

15 For what I am doing, I do not understand. For what I will to do, that I do not practice; but what I hate, that I do.

16 If, then, I do what I will not to do, I agree with the law that it is good.

17 But now, it is no longer I who do it, but sin that dwells in me.

18 For I know that in me (that is, in my flesh) nothing good dwells; for to will is present with me, but how to perform what is good I do not find.

19 For the good that I will to do, I do not do; but the evil I will not to do, that I practice.

20 Now if I do what I will not to do, it is no longer I who do it, but sin that dwells in me.

How can the Apostle Paul say, "It is not I, but sin that dwells in me?" It's the same reason **1 John 3:9** says:

Whoever has been born of God does not sin, for His seed remains in him; and he cannot sin, because he has been born of God.

Your inner man cannot sin. It is born of God, is in God, and has the life of God. Nothing in God can sin. That's why sin draws our minds out of faith and into the flesh. The body of sin wars to take over our minds to gratify its desires. But this is only possible when our spiritual life is weak. Look again at **Romans 7:21-23**

21 I find then a law, that evil is present with me, the one who wills to do good.

22 For I delight in the law of God according to the inward man.

23 But I see another law in my members, warring against the law of my mind, and bringing me into captivity to the law of sin which is in my members.

Sin in your members (or body of flesh) wars against your mind so you set your mind on things of the flesh again. It could be lust, or it could be self-glorification through religion. The flesh wants to be affirmed and gratified, but it can only do so when the mind is under its influence.

Notice that even when Paul spoke about losing is battle against sin, he still said that the inner man delights in the law of God. Flesh delights in sin. Look at his final conclusion in **Romans 7:25**

I thank God—through Jesus Christ our Lord! So then, with the mind I myself serve the law of God, but with the flesh the law of sin.

In the flesh, you can only serve sin, but you have been given the power of the Spirit. The mind on the Spirit serves God by nature. Its nature is a partaker of God's nature, so your inner man has the same desires as God. If you learn to walk according to the Spirit, you don't have to worry about trying to obey God. It's in your nature to do so. It is only when you are in the flesh that sin is a threat. Even so, once you are walking by faith again, the flesh has no power over you. Let's end this chapter with this amazing promise from **Galatians 5:**

[16] I say then: Walk in the Spirit, and you shall not fulfill the lust of the flesh.

[17] For the flesh lusts against the Spirit, and the Spirit against the flesh; and these are contrary to one another, so that you do not do the things that you wish.

[18] But if you are led by the Spirit, you are not under the law.

You don't have to worry about sin. You don't have to worry about lust. You don't have to worry about anger, jealousy, greed, or any other temptation of the flesh. If you walk in the Spirit, you WILL NOT fulfill the desires of the flesh. The flesh loses all influence and power.

To help ease our concerns, this passage ends with the affirmation, "If you are led by the Spirit, you are not under the law."

The law is for the sinner; not for the spiritual man or woman. The law becomes irrelevant because sin has become irrelevant. You don't need a law to prevent sin in the life of someone who has no desire to sin.

When I walk through a nursery, no rule keeper is following me around to make sure I don't steal dolls. They are of no interest to me. A young child has to be told, "Put away the toys. You can't take that out of daycare." But an adult does not. They don't because they have matured so far beyond toddler toys that there is no temptation.

The Apostle Paul said, "When I was a child, I thought as a child. I acted as a child. But when I became a man, I put away childish things."

The truth is, you mature out of sin. When I became an adult, no one had to tell me to put away the romper stompers I played with when I watched Romper Room as a child. Somewhere along the way, I lost the desire without anyone telling me it was time to grow up.

When I was a young teen, I went with my mother to visit her friend. She had a son who wanted to show me his toys. I walked in the room and saw a wonderful collection of toys that I would have loved to have had as a child. For a moment, they were appealing. I tinkered with a cool looking castle that had every accessory one could imagine. It was quite a toy, but try as I might, I could not keep my interest going.

I wasn't very old, and I remember being surprised that these great toys had no satisfaction. Within a few minutes, I was ready to move on.

Sin in the Christian life is the same way. To keep someone in the immaturity of the flesh, and say, "Don't touch that. You can't do that. You have to behave this way," is foolish. They are trying to resist what they desire, and force themselves to do what they are not yet capable of accomplishing.

If we mature in the Spirit, no one has to tell us to quit sinning. Sometimes a growing Christian will fall back into an old sin. That's because it looks good and we remember how much we liked sin before Christ. But in a short time, we'll realize that it doesn't satisfy. It no longer quenches our desires. Yet, because we don't know how to meet our inner need, we keep tampering with sin, hoping something will satisfy.

The truth is, stop worrying about sin. Stop worrying about whether someone else will sin. As we (and they) learn to mature in the Spirit, sin becomes a worthless relic from the past. We leave it behind because we are now a man or woman who has put away childish things.

If we keep teaching elementary things, we will keep others in the elementary mindset. Hebrews 6 begins by saying, "Therefore, leaving the discussion of the elementary principles of Christ, let us go on to perfection, not laying again the foundation of repentance from dead works and of faith toward God, of the doctrine of baptisms, of laying on of hands, of resurrection of the dead, and of eternal judgment."

Leave behind the elementary things. It's not about the law; it's about reaching toward the perfection of Christ. Leave behind the perpetual repentance mindset, and go on toward perfection. Galatians 4:9 calls the law 'the weak and beggarly things that create bondage'. It then asks the church why they want to return to this instead of thriving in the Spirit's affirmation that God is now our 'Abba' or 'Daddy'.

We are no longer walking in fear and judgment, but in a loving and nurturing relationship where the Spirit of God matures us out of the flesh, instead of judging us in the flesh.

You have escaped the flesh and all its weaknesses. Press on toward maturity and learn to walk by grace through faith. Then the flesh loses all power, and your life in the Spirit operates in God's power. The same power that raised Christ from the dead has been given to you as a gift of grace.

All things are yours. Sin is dead. A fruitful Christian life is a guarantee. Believe!

Discussion Questions

Review Galatians 2:20. What is the difference between living for Christ, and allowing Christ to live through you?

Read Micah 7:19 and Galatians 5:16. Who's job is it to subdue sin in your life?

Review Romans 8:3-8. What does it mean to be carnally (or fleshly) minded?

How does the Christian fulfill the law?

What is the difference between godly sorrow and worldly sorrow, in regards to sin?

What does the word 'sanctified' mean?

Review 1 Thessalonians 5:23, 1 Corinthians 6:11, and Hebrews 10:10. Why does the Bible say we are sanctified, but then say, "May the Lord sanctify you completely, body, soul, and spirit?

Read Romans 8:11. Where does the power to conform our outward life to a godly standard come from?

Why don't more Christians experience this life?

Why is trying to serve God by human effort an act of the flesh?

How do we do works without trusting in human effort?

Review Colossians 2:11-12. What is the circumcision made without hands?

If we have a new nature that cannot sin, where does sin come from?

If we are struggling with sinful tendencies, how do we change our behavior?

If the Bible says that whoever is born of God cannot sin, why do we sin?

How do we outgrow sin?

Should we be warning people not to sin, or teaching them how to grow in the faith?

Explain the difference between the life in the flesh and the life in the Spirit.

Overcoming Addictive Behavior

Now that we've examined the flesh versus the Spirit, we need to carry that understanding into our daily lives. We all have addictions. Some are socially acceptable, while others are not. Some addictions of the flesh are more destructive than others. Addictions are just the cravings of the flesh. The flesh craves to be fed, affirmed, acknowledged, gratified, and satisfied.

The truth is, you can never satisfy the flesh. The Bible says, "The eyes of man are never satisfied."[21] This is true. A few years back there was a survey that asked people how much money they needed to be satisfied with their income. The person making $20,000 said they needed 40. The person making $40,000 said 80. Across the economic scale, nearly every person said they needed double what they were making in order to feel satisfied. John D. Rockefeller, one of the richest men in history, was asked how much was enough? He said, "Just a little bit more."

This is the nature of the flesh. No matter what appeals to your desire, gratifying it will never create satisfaction. Gratification is the temporary satiation of a desire. It is the point when we've consumed enough to temporarily stop the desire. Sometimes it's the point where we loathe our desire. But satisfaction remains strangely absent.

A person with an eating disorder doesn't stop when the need for nourishment is fulfilled. They are driven by the desire to find satisfaction in the food. Yet the more they consume, the less they feel satisfaction in this life. The same is true for sexual addictions, greedy addictions, addictions of rage, and substance addictions.

Have you ever met a satisfied alcoholic? Or drug user? Addictions that require money are quicker in their destruction, but in the heart, every addiction is destructive. Happiness can't be found in satisfying the flesh. Even religion can be an addiction.

---

[21] Proverbs 27:20

A friend had a boyfriend addicted to religion. Without any apparent rationale, he would demand his girlfriend to stop everything she was doing and go into a quiet room to pray. It happened so often, the family felt like he considered them to be unclean. On one family gathering, he demanded to separate for prayer 5 or 6 times in the space of a few hours.

The relationship ended when he was caught trying to molest a child in the family. His religious addiction was the outward sign of an inner struggle. He tried to cleanse his impure desires with religion, and the more his desires grew, the more obsessed he was with religious practices.

Substituting one addiction for another is not the solution. Having been someone who came out of addiction, I know that religious practices did not remove my desires. I tried to cover them for a while, but when the inner cravings awoke, I was powerless to stop them.

I grew up being taught that the flesh was strong, but I had to be stronger. I had to will myself to do right and will myself not to do wrong. The flesh is not strong. The flesh is weak. Look at the words of Jesus in **Matthew 26:41**

"Watch and pray, lest you enter into temptation. The spirit indeed *is* willing, but the flesh *is* weak."

This was not a call to trust in the act of praying, but for the disciples to pray to receive the strength of the Spirit. It was to take the focus off themselves and trust in the Lord. During the time of prayer, the disciples fell asleep. During Jesus' time of prayer, He received strength. They were trying to will themselves into prayer, but Jesus was praying, "Not My will, but Yours."

Four times in the New Testament, we are told that the flesh is weak. It appears strong to us because it controls our desires – at least it does so when we are living through the flesh. I'd like to change your perspective.

You were created for righteousness. You were created by God for fellowship with God. Not religion, but fellowship. The Bible says that Moses spoke face to face with God, as a man speaks with his friend. That is God's intent and desire for you. God is not concerned with your religion or any effort you make to appease Him. God wants you to know Him as both a Father and a friend.

A child sees their dad as an authoritative figure. As a child, Dad made me obey. He corrected me when I went astray. My mother was the same. But as I grew into adulthood, the relationship began to change. The more mature I became, the more our relationship became a friendship, and parenthood faded away.

The same is true with God. To the child of the faith, God corrects, instructs, guides, and works to mature. If we stay in immaturity, the relationship never gets beyond the parent-child perspective. God's purpose is to mature me in the Spirit so that I can mature spiritually. As maturity happens, I become a spiritual man, and the relationship grows into an intimate friendship. As I outgrow the flesh, those hindrances fall away.

The Bible says, "God is Spirit, and those who worship must do so in Spirit and truth." The same is true with fellowship. A carnal man or woman cannot relate to God, who is Spirit. A spiritually maturing man or woman will see barriers between them and God fall away as fellowship emerges.

God is working in your life to get the flesh suppressed so you can discover true life and satisfaction. Satisfaction is only found in the life of the Spirit. This is because we were created for spiritual fellowship. A carnal man is stuck in weakness, but a spiritual man is free.

By spiritual, I am referring to the life in the Spirit. Many people call themselves spiritual, but we are talking about a life that walks in the Spirit. The flesh is weak, so it must decrease that the life of the Spirit may increase.

The flesh isn't strong; it's weak. It only has power because your spiritual life is weaker. I'm going to say something most people have a hard time accepting – at least until they understand the flesh versus the Spirit. You cannot defeat your flesh. You cannot fix your flesh. You cannot overcome your flesh. You can only outgrow your flesh. You can't fix yourself. You can either grow out or be trapped in the cycle of substituting one fleshly habit for another.

Some habits appear to be good, but they are still teaching us to trust in the flesh. When someone uses coping mechanisms, or seeks out less destructive habits, the best they can hope for is a less destructive form of the flesh.

The flesh is weak. You were created to live as a spiritual man or woman, but the flesh is too weak to accomplish that purpose. Instead of the flesh dragging you down, what is actually happening is the flesh has given its best shot, and doesn't have the strength to continue.

When a recovering alcoholic returns to the bottle, we call it 'falling off the wagon.' It is a fall. It isn't the flesh winning a battle against your will. It is the flesh losing the battle because it is incapable of sustaining the will.

The Bible calls us 'More than conquerors through Christ.' You are already a conqueror in the Spirit. The flesh can't conquer the Spirit, but if our spirit is weak, we will yield our minds back to the flesh. Once the flesh is in control of the mind, our will is already under siege.

The way to victory is to have a thriving life in the Spirit. As your spirit grows into maturity, the weaknesses of the flesh lose their power. I spent more than twenty years of my Christian life trying to overcome my sinful addiction, and my success was limited to the weakness of the flesh. I tried to overcome through the flesh, but because the flesh is weak, my success was always short-lived.

When I finally began to understand God's acceptance of me, and I quit listening to preachers who told me that God was angry at my sins, and I was back under condemnation, things began to change. The more I understood my acceptance, the more I learned to return to the life of the Spirit, instead of running from God. Then as I matured, my weaknesses began to fall away.

My flesh was too weak to attain to the life of the Spirit. Religious efforts could not strengthen my flesh, and when I tired, I fell back into the sins I hated. The flesh has not been empowered to live for God. Our spirit has. Our flesh is not called to rule us, but we it. And we can only rule the flesh by walking in the Spirit, then God's power subdues the flesh.

I outgrew sin. I am still outgrowing sin. The more I grow in my spirit, the more sin falls away. Strongholds are only in the flesh. The life in the Spirit is without chains.

Let me share another secret with you. As you begin maturing, there will be times when you fall back into the flesh. When a toddler starts walking, they fall. They fall often. But as they grow, the falls become less frequent.

When my kids were learning to walk, they had a lot of bruises. Their shins were bruised from stumbling into things. Sometimes they would get a knot on their forehead when they fell and hit a chair. But they didn't decide to stay with crawling around.

As you start growing spiritually, you will fall. Sometimes it will hurt. Sometimes you'll feel frustrated. But God is not angry when you stumble and fall. I didn't yell at my toddlers for falling. I praised them for their success. I can tell you that I am not a better parent than God. If I rejoiced when my children succeeded, and said, "It's okay," when they fell, would God do less?

When my kids banged their heads, I picked them up and comforted them. I never scolded them for their lack of perfection. Do we now think God is less of a parent than we are? No. When you fall, God is not chiding you; He's carrying you. Religion scolds you, but God comforts, encourages, and calls you to grow. Even more, as you learn to trust Him, He does something no parent can do, gives you the strength to press on.

Maturity is not instant. It takes time. It takes nourishment. We feed on the goodness of the Lord, and the scriptures are an important part of our spiritual nourishment.

We grow in the word as we study and hear it taught. This is one reason why it's important to be around teachers that understand the love of God. Anyone who teaches fear and condemnation to the believer does not understand what Christ has accomplished for us. But as the word is taught in the Spirit, the Holy Spirit gives us revelation. That means God opens our understanding. Then as we read the word, we are seeking more revelation. But God will not reveal more than our ability to receive. The more we grow, the more God reveals.

A kindergartener could never understand trigonometry. To teach it would be foolish. They have to know numbers before they can count. They have to count before they can add, and so on. Yet when it comes to spiritual growth, we expect instant success or we feel frustrated. Add to this, when we are taught what we should be, but not the spiritual path of maturity to get there, we feel defeated.

No kindergartener is scolded by a teacher because they should know algebra. They don't tell a first-grader, "Look at that engineer. That's what we should all be able to do." Instead we tell them, "You can be anything you want to be, but you have to learn."

So why do we scold our congregations and say, "Look at Christ. This is what you should be?" Why do we beat people down for what they are not, instead of saying, "This is what you can be?"

The truth is, you have the open door before you. God has opened the door through Christ. He bore your sins, took upon Himself your penalty, and all your judgment was satisfied through Christ. There is no more judgment. According to the Bible, you have escaped wrath (against sin) through Him.[22] Now there is no condemnation to those who are in Christ Jesus.[23]

It's time to stop looking at sin, and start looking at the gift of righteousness. It's time to stop looking at failure, and start looking at the promise that you are already a conqueror. It's time to stop looking at the flesh, and look at the life of the Spirit.

It does not matter what your addiction is. It has been defeated. It doesn't matter what you have done, it was in the flesh, but you are of the Spirit. The Bible says that all things are possible to those who believe.[24] It's time to start believing what God has declared over you. As you believe, start walking in it. When you struggle and doubt comes in, walk in faith in what you do not yet see. Look at **Hebrews 11:1**

---

[22] Romans 5:9
[23] Romans 8:1, 9
[24] Matthew 9:23

Now faith is the assurance of things hoped for, the evidence of things not seen.

You have been given the assurance of God's love, and the victory of your spiritual perfection. You may not see this in your life, but walk by faith in that hope. Hope is the trust in what God has declared, knowing it is true before you see it. When you fail, walk in faith, the assurance of what God has promised. Then what you do not yet see will become a reality.

The person with hope in God will fall, but will always get up and begin walking by faith again. They know that God is maturing them, not condemning them. They learn to lean on God and trust Him when they are weak. The faithless says, "God is angry at my failures and sins," but the man or woman of faith says, "God has already forgiven all my sins, and He has the power to defeat my flesh."

As you mature in your spirit, friendship with God emerges and the flesh loses power. The very addictions and weaknesses that control your life today will become irrelevant as you mature. You won't have to work to overcome. As you grow in the faith, you will walk in His overcoming power, and the flesh falls powerlessly into the past.

It's all about His power in your life, your trust in both His power, and His absolute love for you.

Discussion Questions

How long do life events make you happy? (i.e. a new car, house, vacation, pay raise)

Why does happiness fade so quickly?

What does the Bible mean by, "The spirit is willing, but the flesh is weak?"

Read 2 Corinthians 12:7-10. How does this help us to understand how to overcome our struggles?

How is this different from the expert advice we see in the secular world and in many Christian circles?

How does parenthood give us a glimpse into how God helps us to mature in the faith?

Is the flesh strong or weak?

Why does the flesh overcome us?

Why do Christians have short-lived success when they try to rise above their weaknesses?

How is walking in the Spirit different than turning over a new leaf?

When a Christian is just beginning to learn to walk, does God lash out at them in anger when they stumble?

If we are teaching people that God's wrath burns at every stumble, are we presenting a heavenly Father that is less loving than an earthly father?

Can we know the deep things of God without following the path of maturity? Explain your answer.

Review Hebrews 11:1. Explain what this means in your life.

When a Christian falls, how does God react?

When you fall, how do you view your relationship with God?

How should you view your relationship with God?

The Crucified Life

When Jesus began sharing His coming crucifixion, Peter rebuked Him by saying, "Far be it from You, Lord. This shall not happen to you." At this point, Jesus turned to Peter and said, "Get behind Me Satan...for you are not mindful of the things of God, but of men."

Of course, Jesus wasn't calling Peter 'Satan'. He was standing against the devil's influence over Peter. Peter's opposition was understandable, for we do the same things. We look at the comfort of this life as the evidence of God's favor, but there are times when the temporal stands in the way of the eternal. The thought of Jesus suffering was an offense to Peter, but Peter's desire to protect Jesus was an offense to Jesus.

Without the death of Jesus in the flesh, there would be no life given through the Spirit. When Jesus began His ministry, John the Baptist said, "He must increase, but I must decrease." In the same way, the life of the Spirit must increase, but our life in the flesh must decrease.

After rebuking Peter's desire to protect Christ, Jesus teaches us about the crucified life. Look at **Matthew 16:24-25**

24 Then Jesus said to His disciples, "If anyone desires to come after Me, let him deny himself, and take up his cross, and follow Me.
25 "For whoever desires to save his life will lose it, but whoever loses his life for My sake will find it.

Taking up our cross is not the call to suffer. Many have said, "This is my cross to bear," when they have pain in this life. Indeed, we may go through suffering, but the call to take up the cross is not God instructing us to find a way to suffer. It's the call to die to the flesh so we can find true life in the Spirit. In Jesus' interaction with Peter, He goes on to teach the following: **John 12:24-25**

24 "Most assuredly, I say to you, unless a grain of wheat falls into the ground and dies, it remains alone; but if it dies, it produces much grain.

[25] "He who loves his life will lose it, and he who hates his life in this world will keep it for eternal life.

Jesus is teaching a dual illustration. He is pointing to His coming death, burial, and resurrection, but He is also equating this with our life in the Spirit. The flesh must die so our life in the Spirit can emerge. We take up our cross by dying to the flesh in Christ. Everything in this life is passing. Not one worldly accomplishment or possession will translate into eternity.

The Bible says that God's ways and thoughts are higher than man's ways and thoughts,[25] and the ways of God are foolishness to the natural human way of thinking.[26] We look at human desires and think we can find happiness, but it always eludes us. We look at our ways and think we can fit God into our life and plans, but contentment and true success is never found there. It is natural to look at our ways and say, "I can do this for God," but rarely does this align with God's purposes. God doesn't take our works and inhabit them. God reveals His works and invites us to enter what He has purposed.

To die to our will appears foolish. Even to the church, the way of faith is scoffed at. We talk about walking by faith, but once we decide to truly step out in faith, friends and family will warn us that it isn't practical. No man has ever been praised by the world or carnally minded Christians for stepping away from a lucrative career to follow God.

This is why many in the church seek God's will for their lives, but remain unsatisfied and unfulfilled. God's will is to die to the flesh so He can raise us up in the Spirit. It is to die to our will, so God can raise us up into His eternal will.

We see an example of this in the life of Jesus. The night He was betrayed, Jesus separated from the crowd to pray. Three times Jesus prayed for the cup of suffering to pass from Him. In His humanity, the dread of the cross became real, and the stress of facing His suffering was great.

---

[25] Isaiah 55:9
[26] 1 Corinthians 1:18, 1 Corinthians 2:14

The Bible says that though Jesus was the Son, He learned obedience to the Father by the things He suffered.[27] This is referring to the evening before He was arrested. He began His prayer in the flesh by saying, "If it is possible, let this cup [of suffering] pass from Me." But He ended in the Spirit by shifting His focus from the suffering of the flesh to the power of the Spirit as He prayed, "Nevertheless, not My will, but Yours."

Jesus' will was to escape the suffering of the cross. He had to die to His will so the eternal will of God could emerge. Three times Jesus prayed for an escape, and each time He shifted His focus to the eternal purpose He came to fulfill. An amazing thing happened when He died to His own will. Luke 22:43 says that an angel from heaven strengthened Him.

The power of heaven is given as we die to the flesh. Jesus didn't try to make His will change. He died to His will. The Bible says that though Jesus was fully God, He veiled His glory and came in the likeness of man.[28] His strength is the same strength we have. He walked in the power of the Holy Spirit, just as we do.

You and I often face the challenge of our will versus God's will. We falter because we are trying to make the will of the flesh align with the will of God. It can't. It must die. Like Christ, we also must say, "Not my will, but Yours."

The cross tried to capture Jesus' mind, but His strength didn't come from defeating His fear of the cross. It came from the joy before Him. The Bible says, "The joy of the Lord is our strength."[29] Jesus proved this. The Bible also says that Jesus is our example. For the joy set before Him, Jesus endured the cross while despising its shame.

He endured because of the joy beyond the cross. Jesus looked past the suffering to your redemption. You were the encouragement for Jesus to endure. He saw your forgiveness, reconciliation, and fellowship of love with Him, and the joy of

---

[27] Hebrews 5:8
[28] Philippians 2:6-7
[29] Nehemiah 8:10

winning your soul gave Christ the strength to endure what He hated.

The Bible tells us to look to Jesus so we don't become discouraged in our souls.[30] We also will have the strength to endure the struggles of our lives if we find the joy of the Lord, by looking beyond our suffering to the fulfillment of God's promise to us.

Like a grain of wheat, your flesh dies, so the life of the Spirit can emerge. Look at a seed. It is lifeless, dry, and fruitless. Think about a dried up corn kernel. If you didn't know better, you'd say that it could never become alive. But when it is put into the ground, it absorbs the moisture around it, dies to itself, and a sprout emerges. The old kernel quickly withers away as the new plant grows.

You also die to the flesh, are buried with Christ, you are watered by the Spirit through baptism, and new life emerges where a dried soul once was. As you learn to grow in the Spirit, your old life of the flesh withers into the past, and maturity begins. Look at **Romans 6:4-7**

> 4 Therefore we were buried with Him through baptism into death, that just as Christ was raised from the dead by the glory of the Father, even so we also should walk in newness of life.
> 5 For if we have been united together in the likeness of His death, certainly we also shall be *in the likeness* of *His* resurrection,
> 6 knowing this, that our old man was crucified with *Him*, that the body of sin might be done away with, that we should no longer be slaves of sin.
> 7 For he who has died has been freed from sin.

Until you die to yourself, you are trapped in a body of sin. But by faith, you enter into Christ's death, the old nature (or old man) is nailed to the cross, and you are resurrected into new life. This is what Jesus means by 'take up your cross and follow Me.'

---

[30] Hebrews 12:1-3

The Crucified Life

When you enter the life of the Spirit by faith, you are entering into Jesus' accomplished works. You are entering into His death so you can be raised into His life. Then once you die, sin has no more power over you. You who have died have been set free from sin. Let's continue looking at this amazing truth in **Romans 6:8-11**

> 8 Now if we died with Christ, we believe that we shall also live with Him,
> 9 knowing that Christ, having been raised from the dead, dies no more. Death no longer has dominion over Him.
> 10 For *the death* that He died, He died to sin once for all; but *the life* that He lives, He lives to God.
> 11 Likewise you also, reckon yourselves to be dead indeed to sin, but alive to God in Christ Jesus our Lord.

Just as Jesus died to sin once for all, but now lives to God, you also reckon (or account) yourself the same. You are dead indeed to sin, but alive to God in Christ.

The promise is that you are dead indeed. Not maybe. Not once you get your act together. It is an accomplished fact. You are dead indeed to sin. You are alive indeed to God. Yet until you reckon this to be true, it profits you nothing. To reckon is to believe and account this to be true for you. It is by promise, not by works. There is nothing you can do to make this happen. It has already been accomplished. But until you believe this, it won't be a reality in your life.

Regarding God's promise, the Bible gives us the example of the people from the Exodus. The Promised Land was already theirs. It was given by promise, and all God required was for them to believe in God's power to fulfill the promise. The giants of the land challenged their faith, but the only role of their enemies was to prove the people's faith. God said the promise was theirs, but they had to enter the promise by faith.

The people missed the blessing because they trusted in their weaknesses instead of God. They trusted in the enemy instead of God. They trusted in failure, circumstances, and the oppositions that stood between them and the promise. Then God said, "You will not enter My rest."

Scripture teaches that this is our example. We are called to trust in God and rest in the promise. Not one of God's people in the Old Testament did anything to earn the promise. They weren't allowed in because they were good, nor were they denied the promise because of their sins. The next generation entered the promise for one reason – they followed Joshua into the promise. Joshua is a picture of Christ. The name 'Joshua' means, Jehovah is Salvation. The name 'Jesus' means, Jehovah is Salvation. Jehovah is the name God gave to the Old Testament people to identify Himself.

The New Testament says that the same gospel preached to the people who missed the promise of God was also preached to us, but it didn't profit them because it was not mixed with faith.[31]

God required one thing of the people – trust in His power to fulfill His promises to them. God requires one thing of you and I, to trust in His power to fulfill His promises to us. He promised to suppress our iniquities and forgive our sins. He promised to give us the gift of His righteousness, and the power of the Spirit to transform us into Christ's likeness – spirit, soul, and body.

God did not promise to give us these things after we work for them, or after we work sin out of our lives. The person who does not trust in God's righteousness will try to produce their own. The person who does not believe in the life of the Spirit will not allow themselves to be crucified with Christ. Yet until we die to the flesh through the crucifixion of Christ, we can't live in the life of the Spirit. Look now at **Galatians 2:20-21**

> [20] "I have been crucified with Christ; it is no longer I who live, but Christ lives in me; and the *life* which I now live in the flesh I live by faith in the Son of God, who loved me and gave Himself for me.
> [21] "I do not set aside the grace of God; for if righteousness *comes* through the law, then Christ died in vain."

---

[31] Hebrews 4:2

How many people in the church set aside the grace of God and try to become righteous for Him? How many are trying to live for Christ instead of allowing Christ to live through them?

It is not you who live for Christ, it is Christ that lives through you. Righteousness is the life of Christ in you. Your lifestyle becomes acceptable to God when you stop trying to do for God, and allow the Spirit to flow through you.

If you try to keep the law, you are calling Jesus' death on the cross a worthless (or vain) act. The Bible says that Jesus became sin for us that we might become the righteousness of God in Him.[32] You are not trying to become righteous. You ARE the righteousness of God if you are in Christ. Everything we add to God's righteousness is a pollution, not a purification.

By faith you must reckon, or account, this to be true. Believe you are dead to sin – even when you blow it. Put off your trust in the gratification of the flesh. All sin is based on trusting in the flesh instead of God. Put your trust back in God and reckon yourself dead indeed to sin. Believe this is true – even if your eyes cannot yet see the reality of God's declaration. Don't refuse the promise because you have giants in your flesh. They are nothing.

Reckon yourself to be alive to God in Christ. It's an accomplished fact. You have the life of the Spirit, and it is by promise, not by what you do or don't do. It is by faith – trusting in what God has revealed in His word. He has already declared you clean. And what God has called clean, you are not to call unclean.[33]

You have been made clean through the sacrifice of Christ. You are called to trust in His work, receive it by faith, and believe what God has declared, even if the natural mind can't understand this. As you receive the crucified life, you will see the resurrected life emerging. Account yourself dead to sin – even if you sin. Account yourself alive in God's righteousness – even if you have done nothing to deserve it. It's all about God's works, and trusting in what He has done.

---

[32] 2 Corinthians 5:21
[33] Acts 10:15

The Crucified Life

Discussion Questions

Review Matthew 16:24-25. What does it mean to take up your cross and follow Christ.

Review John 12:24-25. Explain what this passage means for your life.

Does God call us to submit our plans for Him to bless? Explain.

Read Hebrews 12:1-3. How did Jesus feel about the cross?

What gave Him the strength to endure?

Can you have joy when your circumstances are not happy?

Review Romans 6:4-7. Explain how this applies to the Christian life.

Review Romans 6:8-11. What does it mean to reckon yourself dead indeed to sin?

If someone believes sin is alive, or has power, how does this affect their Christian walk?

How does reckoning sin to be dead affect us when we do sin?

Why does God put us to the test before we receive the greatest of His promises?

Review Galatians 2:20-21. Explain the difference between living for God, and allowing Christ to live through you.

Is righteousness and the life of the Spirit based on what you do or don't do? Explain.

The Resurrected Life

The lack of understanding of the resurrected life is why people claim that living in grace is a life that tolerates sin. In truth, this is the only life that overcomes sin. Trusting in legalism does not work. When the Christian life is dependent upon our ability to resist temptation, or our ability to keep religious rules, there may be moments of success, but it is limited at best.

An opponent of grace accused me of having secret sin in my life, for anyone who trusts in grace must be trying to justify sin. The irony is that when I trusted in a legalistic form of Christianity, I had many secret sins. I tried to cover them with good works and self-delusions of righteousness. In a quest to condemn my own sins, I was very critical of others.

This is why I often say that legalism either creates despair or self-delusion. It never creates righteousness. I can only grade myself on a curve, or be driven to despair by the truth that I was defeated by the law. Since **James 2:10** says that if we keep the whole law but offend in one single point, we are guilty of the whole law, legalism is an impossible standard. Not only that, but mixing law back into grace does nothing more than introduce condemnation back into the Christian's life.

Legalism forces me to ignore this truth or be driven to the reality that the law is my condemner – regardless of how religious I am, or how many works I do.

The resurrected life changes this. Because I have been raised with Christ as a new creation through the life of the Spirit, the law has no jurisdiction over me, and sin has no power. The strength of sin is the law, and because I am no longer under the law, there is nothing to empower sin. Now I only have the choice to walk according to the flesh, where nothing good dwells, or walk according to the Spirit, where nothing evil dwells.

The resurrected life is the normal Christian life. Yet because the church teaches through the flesh, attempts to live out their faith through the flesh, and views the word of God through the flesh, the abnormal life of the flesh has become so common place that we don't see it as abnormal.

Believing in the grace of Christ does not equate to disobedience. It's the only way to live in obedience. We live in the Spirit, which is always in agreement with God. We obey from a position of holiness. Outside of Christ, people attempt to obey from a position of the flesh in an effort to obtain holiness, which is impossible.

The life of the flesh may have religious zeal, but it has misdirected enthusiasm. Religious zeal often tries to force others to conform to a religious standard. But the Spirit led life invites others to join them in the better way of life. Fleshly-minded religion tries to force people to stop sinning, but the Spirit invites people into righteousness.

The Bible never tells the church to force morality on the worldly culture around them. When the New Testament speaks of sin, it explains to the church that they are no longer of the flesh. The world is of the flesh and has no godly foundation to build upon. To demand a sinner to stop sinning is an impossible demand. The only way to force morality on a culture is to oppress, but even that does not change the heart. Religiously oppressed people will only conform outwardly as long as the fear of consequences is present. Once the opportunity to rebel presents itself, there will be a mass exodus, and sinful man will return to his natural state.

We evangelize by calling people out of the flesh. Holding up a sign that says, 'Repent or burn,' does not change the heart of any. Even if someone is driven to the altar by fear, their repentance is of the flesh and cannot sustain them for long. Without a change of nature, manipulating people into repentance is nothing more than a form of oppression.

When the Apostle Paul encountered a nation filled with idolatry and monuments to various gods, he did not scold them for their sins. Idolatry was not their problem – it was merely a symptom of the problem. So Paul didn't start with rebuking idolatry. Instead he began with their temple dedicated to an unknown god, and began to unveil Jesus as the God they were searching for.

But to the church he says, "Do not become idolaters,"[34] and "Keep yourselves from idols."[35] When speaking of idolatry and other sins, the Bible says the following **1 Corinthians 6:11**

> And such were some of you. But you were washed, but you were sanctified, but you were justified in the name of the Lord Jesus and by the Spirit of our God.

This was not only the warning of idolatry, but the Bible goes on to list all the sins of the flesh that we see in the culture. From greed, to idolatry, to sexual sins, to covetousness, the Bible calls us to avoid falling back into the sins we have escaped from. The resurrected life does not have these temptations, but the flesh is always under temptation.

The call of obedience is to the people of the church, who have already been washed, sanctified, and justified by the power of the Spirit. It is not the culture of the world that is under this call. Their call is to come and experience the life of the Spirit. Our mission is to go into the world and present the life of Christ.

A church that is not experiencing the life of the Spirit will not have the understanding to present Christ to the culture in an effective way. Modern evangelism focuses on wrath and judgement in order to create fear. That makes the gospel appear to be a threat instead of a call to the abundant life. Telling people that serving God is better than burning in hell is not the gospel.

Jesus presented the abundant life to people with the call to repent. We have lost the meaning of repentance. It does not mean to grovel in guilt. It does not even mean to confess sin. The word repentance is the Greek word 'metanoia', which means to change the mind, or to change one's purpose. Look at the words of **Romans 2:4**

---

[34] 1 Corinthians 10:7
[35] 1 John 5:21

Or do you despise the riches of His goodness, forbearance, and longsuffering, not knowing that the goodness of God leads you to repentance?

Romans 2 is written to the religious zealot that condemns others. Those who condemn others are condemning themselves, for we are all guilty of the same things.[36] This is when the question is thrown out, "Do you not know that it's the goodness of God that leads you to repentance?"

The goodness of God is what invites people to leave the flesh and come out of the world and into the life of the Spirit. Shouting from a bullhorn, "Look at your sin," does not lead to true repentance, for it is not calling people to look at the gift of God. Some teach (and I also once taught) that people have to see their sin before they can see their need for Christ. Therefore we must preach against sin. Right?

This is not true. The gospel is not about what we are against, but what we are receiving. Remember our earlier illustration of the man finding the treasure in the field? Once he discovered the treasure, everything he had became worthless. He sold it all to obtain the treasure he had discovered. No one had to say, "Look at your trash." He knew it was worthless once he discovered true value.

It's not our job to convict the world of sin. Jesus said, "The Spirit will convict the world of sin." Our calling is to proclaim the gift of God through Christ. Once the Spirit reveals the truth that Jesus is our treasure, sin will appear to be sin. To condemn what someone treasures does not produce true repentance. To proclaim what is truly valuable is the goodness of God that leads to true repentance.

The same is true for the resurrected life. The church is so consumed with the fear that sin may be among its members that sin becomes the focus. Each week, countless Christians are told, "Look at your sin." We might as well be preaching, "Take your eyes off Jesus and put your focus on your flesh." It doesn't work. The

---

[36] Romans 2:1

churches that preach the hardest against sin may fill up the altars more, but they are not producing sinless Christians. They are producing both frustrated and legalistic Christians. They are producing pride in those who believe they are pleasing God by keeping church rules, and this produces those who condemn others for the same sins that are present in their own lives.

The man who looks at magazines that creates lust will then condemn the man whose lust is in the form of homosexuality. The legalistic Christian reads Romans 1 and it inspires him to draw up a picket sign to protest against homosexuality, but he never recognizes the rest of the sins that apply to himself. What about the immorality of his own lusts? What about covetousness (wanting what someone else has), or envy (resenting when someone else has more, has accomplished something, or has honor we disapprove of). What about strife, backbiting, pride, boasting of your own righteousness, or being unloving and unforgiving.

The fruit of legalism is hypocrisy. The fruit of life in the Spirit is righteousness.

The purpose of the passages that speak against sin is not to arm us to condemn others, but to reveal to us that we are all guilty outside of grace. But the flesh twists the scriptures in ways that justifies ourselves while condemning others. We grade ourselves on a curve, but demand the straight stick of the truth against everyone else. This is why the next chapter continues with the warning, "You who condemn others are condemning yourselves."

Focusing on someone's sin will not bring them to true repentance. Focusing on our own sin will not produce true repentance. There has to be a change of the mind from the flesh to the Spirit. It is the life of the Spirit that defeats sin. The resurrected life IS the life of the Spirit.

You are not called to live in condemnation. That is not repentance. Here is true repentance, **Ephesians 4:22-24**

> [22] that you put off, concerning your former conduct, the old man which grows corrupt according to the deceitful lusts,
> [23] and be renewed in the spirit of your mind,

²⁴ and that you put on the new man which was created according to God, in true righteousness and holiness.

You are not trying to overcome sin. Nor are you trying to re-crucify the flesh. You are not trying to defeat the flesh or overcome your old nature. The old man is dead. You are a new man, a new creation, a person born again in the Spirit. Your natural state is the life of the Spirit.

The flesh calls. The flesh still is in sin, but you are in righteousness. Let's review **Romans 8:9-11**

⁹ But you are not in the flesh but in the Spirit, if indeed the Spirit of God dwells in you. Now if anyone does not have the Spirit of Christ, he is not His.

¹⁰ And if Christ *is* in you, the body *is* dead because of sin, but the Spirit *is* life because of righteousness.

¹¹ But if the Spirit of Him who raised Jesus from the dead dwells in you, He who raised Christ from the dead will also give life to your mortal bodies through His Spirit who dwells in you.

Your flesh is dead in sin. Your spirit is alive in the righteousness of Christ. These two realities are ever with us. Yet there is an amazing promise here. The flesh that is dead in sin can have life – if we are living according to the Spirit. The Spirit will take the life of righteousness and give life to the sinful body of flesh, if we are walking according to faith. The flesh does not have life, it must receive life through the power of the Holy Spirit.

You are no longer of the flesh. If you have received Christ, you already have the resurrected life. Even so, the body is still dead because of sin. Sin still rules our bodies of flesh, and if we are living in the flesh, we are under sins domain. Before coming to Christ, the body ruled us and we had to obey sin. Even our good deeds were acts of the flesh as it sought self-glory and self-righteousness. Sin had dominion over us, but now we have the promise that sin no longer has dominion over our life.[37]

---

[37] Romans 6:14

If we are trying to live out our faith in the flesh, we are submitting back to the body of sin. If we trust in temptation and sin, we are submitting back to the body of sin. Whether we are trying to be righteous through the deadness of the flesh, or are willingly sinning through the flesh, both are fleshly and have no spiritual value. Yet it still has no dominion – other than when we willingly submit to it.

The resurrected life is the person who is a receiver of God's grace and is walking by faith – which is walking in the Spirit. We are not trying to become righteous; we are the righteousness of God through Christ. We are not trying to defeat sin; we are walking in the victory that only is experienced through faith. We don't try to obey; we walk in the obedience of Christ. Look at **2 Corinthians 10:4-5**

> [4] For the weapons of our warfare *are* not carnal but mighty in God for pulling down strongholds,
> [5] casting down arguments and every high thing that exalts itself against the knowledge of God, bringing every thought into captivity to the obedience of Christ,

There is an interesting conflict in some translations with this passage. The more literal translations of the Bible (KJV, NKJV, NASB, etc) say, "To the obedience of Christ". The paraphrased versions tend to say things like, "Make them obey Christ." This is one of those passages where the intent of scripture is very important. Our faith is in Christ, not in our abilities to accomplish religion. Understanding this makes the New Testament much easier to interpret.

The text is not telling Christians to make our thoughts obey Christ. It is a call to dethrone human thinking and trust in the obedience of Jesus – the finished work He gave to us. God said, "As the heavens are higher than the earth, so are My ways higher than your ways, and My thoughts are higher than your thoughts."[38]

We are not fighting with carnal (or fleshly weapons). We don't war according to the flesh in any way. We don't try to force

---

[38] Isaiah 55:9

the world into obedience. We don't try to force ourselves into obedience. We don't even try to force our thoughts into obedience.

One of the most common questions I get is from people who believe they have offended God by thinking a blasphemous thought. People will obsess about their thought life. If you try to master your thought life by human effort, you are empowering the flesh to fight against itself. This can never lead to peace with God.

We are receivers of Jesus' obedience. We take our thoughts captive by surrendering them to the obedience of Christ – which is an act of faith – not of works. When a negative thought pops into your head, trust in the obedience of Christ. Meditate on the Spirit, and the flesh is automatically dethroned.

Have you seen someone being arrested on TV or in person? Sometimes that person mouths off as they are being taken away. They shout threats, insults, and anything else they think will offend. But none of their words have power. They are in handcuffs. They are being led away. They may shout, boast, and threaten, but they are hollow words.

The flesh is the same way. It has been dethroned. When a sinful, or even a blasphemous thought enters our head, we take it captive by trusting in the obedience of Christ. It may continue to echo in our heads, but it is nothing – unless we submit back under it. Our thoughts are already captives. They are cuffed and being led away, but many Christians allow thoughts a place of undo honor by trusting in the condemnation of the enemy. Though they are empty threats that cannot be carried out, people crumble at the feet of these thoughts, and receive them as if they are their own.

You cannot be brought back under condemnation. It is impossible. If you doubt this, go back and reread the first chapter of this book. God has sworn Himself to an oath that He cannot be angry with you again. Once you are in Christ, you have been saved from wrath.[39]

Wrath is off the table. Condemnation is also off the table. There is no condemnation to those who are in Christ.[40] Period.

---

[39] Romans 5:9
[40] Romans 8:1

If this is true, what is the purpose of obedience? Why are we called to obey God if we are already under the obedience of Christ? We are called to obey from a position of righteousness. We are obeying from a position of resting in the obedience of Christ. We are holding fast to what we have been given, so we don't forfeit the abundant life of promise for the empty promises of the flesh.

Take some time to read 1 Corinthians 1. This passage begins by explaining that we have been given all things through Christ, and explains that the goal of these instructions are that we don't come short of any gift.[41]

The goodness of God has revealed His deep love, and calls us to repentance. We believed God, received Christ, and our minds were transformed from a fleshly way of thinking, to a mind that draws from the Spirit, which is the mind of Christ.[42] It is the goodness of God that teaches you how to be a receiver of all things. Because you believe, you trust. Because you trust, you walk by faith.

Why are we now persuaded to take our eyes off the goodness of God, which produces a changed mind (repentance), and place our focus on wrath, sin, and judgment? If the goodness of God transforms our way of thinking into a godly focus, what happens if we focus on sin? Or on wrath? Or on condemnation? Will the anger of God suddenly produce in us a better result than the work of repentance?

When we take our eyes off Christ and start looking at ourselves, we'll begin to see the works of the flesh emerging, instead of the fruit of the Spirit. If we stop looking to and trusting in the obedience of Christ, and replace His obedience with our own human efforts, can we have a mind on the Spirit and bear the fruit of repentance? Absolutely not.

You cannot change yourself. Nor can you maintain your spiritual condition by working to keep yourself by human effort. If the Bible says, "You are saved by grace through faith, and that not of yourselves. It is a gift of God, not of works, so no one can

---

[41] 1 Corinthians 1:7
[42] 1 Corinthians 2:16

boast,"[43] why do we think the Christian life is lived differently than how it is entered? You live the same way you enter the life of the Spirit. The Bible says, "The just shall live by faith."[44]

The Christian life is lived by grace through faith. Everything is a gift of God, not by works so that no one can boast. The resurrected life is the life that lives and walks by faith. You trust in the Spirit; therefore you receive of the Spirit. The life of the Spirit is the work of God, not of man. Let's begin wrapping this chapter up with **Galatians 5:22-23**

> [22] But the fruit of the Spirit is love, joy, peace, longsuffering, kindness, goodness, faithfulness,
> [23] gentleness, self-control. Against such there is no law.

Let me draw a few things to your attention from this passage. The phrase, "Against such there is no law," is not saying that there is no law against these attributes. 'Against' means to be supported by. It can also be translated as, "Through such there is no law." In other words, the fruit of the Spirit does not come through the law. These things are not supported by or dependent upon any law, referring to the Old Covenant law.

The law cannot produce the fruit of the Spirit. This is the purpose for the book of Galatians. The church of Galatia began by faith, but was persuaded by religious Pharisees to return to the Old Testament law. They became legalistic Christians, and the Bible asks the question, "Are you so foolish, having begun by faith, do you now seek to be justified through the law?"

It's the same controversy we face today. Trusting in God for salvation by grace through faith is fine, but once you try to live by grace through faith, the spirit of the Pharisees confronts us, then demands we trust in our ability to keep the law. They wrap it in a thin veneer of faith by using the word 'grace', but the definition of grace is reduced to the claim that we have been given the power to keep the law, instead of trusting in Jesus' fulfillment of the law.

---

[43] Ephesians 2:8-9
[44] Romans 1:7, Galatians 3:11, Hebrews 10:38

The Resurrected Life

It's a subtle shift from trusting in Christ, to trusting in our own works in the name of Christ. It's a shift from praising the glory of God's grace, to glorifying ourselves through works of righteousness, which the Bible condemns.

The natural objections then come up, if this is true, then are we saying the Christian is okay to live in disobedience to God? Are we saying that works are not part of the Christian life? I am saying that human works are not part of the Christian life, but the Spirit does indeed produce the fruit of righteousness and good works.

Read again the passage above from Galatians. Every attribute of the Christian life is the fruit of the Spirit – not the works of the Christian. If the Spirit produces these things in our lives, what are we trying to accomplish? Do we not believe the Spirit has the power to make us into Christ's likeness?

If love is being produced in our lives, will it not drive us to do good to others? If self-control is produced in our lives by the Spirit, do we not believe that self-control will keep us out of sin? What are we trying to accomplish? Why are we trying to do what God has said has already been given?

The resurrected life is the life that walks by faith, focusing on Christ and trusting in the power of the Spirit. As I trust in the life God has given me, I am receiving of the Spirit, and as I am receiving the life of the Spirit, it produces the fruit of the Spirit without my help.

I have never seen a grapevine grunting and straining, and then *pop* a grape emerges. No, the branch rests in the vine, receives the life of the vine, and then fruit is the natural result. A blossom emerges, then falls away to expose the budding fruit. In due time, the fruit ripens and the vine is productive.

This is why Jesus said, "I am the vine, you are the branches. He who abides in me bears much fruit, for without me, you can do nothing."[45] The way of discipleship hasn't changed. All you need to do is learn how to abide in Christ and rest in the Spirit. Jesus is our Sabbath. Sabbath means 'rest'. Take to heart the words of **Hebrews 4:10-11**

---

[45] John 15

The Resurrected Life

¹⁰ For he who has entered His rest has himself also ceased from his works as God *did* from His.

¹¹ Let us therefore be diligent to enter that rest, lest anyone fall according to the same example of disobedience.

Some translations say, "Labor to enter that rest," but the word is 'spoudazo', which means to be diligent, or hasten toward. The word 'labor' as in doing work, is the word 'ergazomai', which means to labor, work, or do business. See John 6:27.

This is a call to pursue the promise of rest. When we see that Christ has completed the work and has become our rest, if we believe, we will rush to enter His rest and cease from our own works. When the people came to Jesus and said, "What must we do to do the works of God," Jesus said, "This is the work of God, that you believe in Him, whom the Father has sent."

This is the work of God, that you believe on Christ, who has already accomplished the works of God, and has invited you to enter rest from your own works by trusting in the finished work of Christ. What's more, those who trust fully in Christ are not only credited with Jesus' works, but the Spirit begins to flow His life into them, and the fruit of the Spirit emerges.

Everything the world and the church are trying to accomplish is already yours. All you must do is believe and enter the work of Christ, where you find rest. The resurrected life is the abundant life that emerges in place of the flesh. If you are trying to resurrect the flesh through either sin or human works of righteousness, you are choking out the resurrected life. But as you rest in faith, life emerges and matures. Then the fruitful life of the Spirit will draw you into good works so you can experience the works of God, and be rewarded as if they were your own.

You can't have the fruit of the Spirit and your life remain fruitless. You can't have the fruit of the Spirit and be overcome by sin. Stop worrying about sin. Stop worrying about doing good works. Make haste to enter His rest, live by faith, and experience the fruitful and victorious Christian life. It is not by human effort, but by faith in Christ alone. We'll end with this wonderful passage from **Philippians 3:9-12**

> [9] and be found in Him, not having my own righteousness, which *is* from the law, but that which *is* through faith in Christ, the righteousness which is from God by faith;
> [10] that I may know Him and the power of His resurrection, and the fellowship of His sufferings, being conformed to His death,

The crucified life leads us directly into the resurrected life. We die to our own efforts. We die to our own righteousness and works. We die to the flesh, knowing that once we have put our trust in His gift of grace, we will also experience the power of His resurrection.

The same power that raised Christ from the dead is in you, and gives life to your physical body. The power of the Spirit suppresses the flesh with all its sins, and gives life to you to live in righteousness. Then the fruit of the Spirit will come out in your life, without any human effort or religious practice on your part. This is the normal Christian life.

The more you learn to live by faith, the more your spirit will mature and become fruitful. It's God's good pleasure to give you His kingdom. That includes the works of the kingdom, life of the Spirit, and joy in your life. Stop trying to become what God has already made you to be. Begin walking in what God has declared over you, and the flesh has no power.

Discussion Questions

Is trying to keep the law an act of faith, or a denial of Christ?

Is obedience an attempt to become holy, or is it God's instructions to keep us from stepping outside of the holiness of the spirit?

Can you find any New Testament scriptures that instructs the church to demand righteousness from the world?

Can the Christian live in holiness without the power of the Holy Spirit?

Can the unbeliever live in holiness without the power of the Holy Spirit?

Explain what biblical repentance means.

Review Ephesians 4:22-24. How does this produce repentance in our lives?

Is there condemnation in this call of repentance?

Read Romans 8:9-11. Where does sin abide?

Where is righteousness from?

Where do we get the power to take the life of righteousness and breathe it into the flesh, which is still dead in sin?

What is the difference between good works through the flesh, and good works through the Spirit?

If the goodness of God leads us to repentance, why do churches focus on wrath, judgment, and fear?

Explain what the Bible means by, "The just shall live by faith."

Read Galatians 5:22-23. What must we do to produce the fruit of the Spirit?

What is the difference between trusting in Christ, and trusting in our efforts for Christ?

Read John 6:28-29. How can believing on Jesus credit us with the works of God?

What is the resurrected life?

The Fruit of Grace

It's time to let go of the false image of an angry God. You are under the New Covenant of grace. It is a covenant, not a condition. A covenant is a binding agreement. God has put Himself under His own oath, which was guaranteed with the blood of Christ. That covenant can't be broken, for it is not dependent upon you. You are not the guarantor of God's covenant.

In Genesis 15, God made a binding covenant with the descendants of Abraham. This became the nation of Israel. It began when Abraham presented his need to God. His wife was barren, past child bearing years, and incapable of providing a son to become an inheritor of what Abraham possessed.

As God promised the land to Abraham, the promise meant little without an heir. To affirm God's word to Abraham, the Lord instructed him to prepare a covenant sacrifice.

In that era, when two people entered a binding contract, they would sacrifice an animal, usually a cow or ram. The animal would be divided in two and laid on each side. The two parties would swear an oath to each other, and walk through the divided animal. The oath was confirmed with each person putting their life up as a guarantee to their part of the covenant. It was a promise, "If I break my part of the covenant, the same will be done to me as was done to this animal."

God commanded Abraham to prepare the sacrifice so the Lord could swear a covenant that Abraham would have a son. His son and his descendants after him would be perpetual heirs of God's promises and this land. Abraham prepared the sacrifice, but something unusual happened. God put Abraham into a deep sleep. God allowed Abraham to see the oath of the covenant through a vision, but he was not permitted to walk through the pieces. Look at **Genesis 15:17-18**

> [17] And it came to pass, when the sun went down and it was dark, that behold, there appeared a smoking oven and a burning torch that passed between those pieces.

¹⁸ On the same day the LORD made a covenant with Abram, saying: "To your descendants I have given this land, from the river of Egypt to the great river, the River Euphrates

Abram was Abraham's name before God changed it. What was the meaning of the oven and torch passing through the pieces? It was God swearing the oath through Christ. Look at **Galatians 3:16-18**

> ¹⁶ Now to Abraham and his Seed were the promises made. He does not say, "And to seeds," as of many, but as of one, "And to your Seed," who is Christ.
> ¹⁷ And this I say, *that* the law, which was four hundred and thirty years later, cannot annul the covenant that was confirmed before by God in Christ, that it should make the promise of no effect.
> ¹⁸ For if the inheritance *is* of the law, *it is* no longer of promise; but God gave *it* to Abraham by promise.

The promise came before the law, and though the law was a covenant, it was a conditional covenant that was dependent upon man's ability to be righteous – which was impossible. Yet the covenant of the law did not nullify the covenant of promise. The law was a covenant between the people and God, but the covenant of promise was outside the law.

The Promised Land belonged to the people by promise, and no sin could nullify the promise. If Abraham had been the guarantee of the covenant, if he fell, or if his descendants fell from God's commands, the covenant would have been broken and the people would have been judged under the demands of the covenant – which was death.

Four-hundred and thirty years later, God gave another covenant to His people. It was the covenant of the law. Unlike the Covenant of Promise, the Covenant of the Law made the people its guarantee. Like the first covenant, it was confirmed with the blood of a sacrifice, warning of judgment for those who broke the covenant, but instead of it being confirmed between God and

Christ, the law was confirmed with the people. When the book of the law was read, Moses sprinkled the book of the law with blood, and then sprinkled the people with the blood.[46]

The covenant of the law was sworn between the law and the people. When a person broke one point of the law, they were guilty, and the law had the right to judge the people. This is why the sacrificial system was given. Instead of imminent death for breaking the covenant, written in the law was an alternate option. A bull or ram could stand in place of the person and bear their judgment. It could not take away sin (see Hebrews 10:4), but it could satisfy the death penalty of breaking the covenant.

But the Covenant of Promise had no provision for an animal sacrifice, for it did not put Abraham or his descendants as guarantees of the covenant. The guarantee was between God and Christ, which we now understand was God the Father and the Son, Jesus Christ. God made a covenant that man could not nullify. Nor could he earn. It was by promise alone.

That was a foreshadow of the coming New Covenant of promise. The Old Covenant was to Abraham and his bloodline – or physical descendants, but this was a shadow of a bigger covenant. The New Covenant is to Abraham's descendants by faith, not bloodline.[47]

Abraham alone prepared the sacrifice of the first covenant. Abraham is the father of the Jews, and the Jewish nation of Israel was the only beneficiary of the Old Covenant. The New Covenant (called the New Testament) was also guaranteed with a blood sacrifice, but this time it would include both Jews, and non-Jews (or Gentiles). The Jewish legal system partnered with the Roman government to condemn Jesus and prepare the sacrifice of the New Covenant.

Once again, man prepared the sacrifice, but was not permitted to become the guarantee of the covenant. The New Covenant was sealed between God the Father and Jesus Christ. Since God is the guarantee of the New Covenant, your sins cannot

---

[46] Exodus 24:6-8
[47] Galatians 3:7, 14

break the covenant of promise. If salvation was dependent upon you making a promise to God, your first sin would break the covenant. But because God could swear by no one greater, He swore by Himself. He made the covenant with Himself, but you are the beneficiary.

Under Abraham, a child was circumcised before he had any ability or understanding so he could enter the covenant of promise. Under Christ, you are circumcised by the removal of your sinful nature before you had any ability or understanding. You do nothing but trust in Christ and allow the Spirit to do His work. You enter the promise by believing the gospel so you can be born again. You enter the promise by faith alone.

This is why God can declare that His forgiveness over you is so secure, that even if the mountains were removed and the stars burn out, His favor will never be withdrawn. His oath that He can never again have wrath against you is because God swore an oath and sealed the covenant with His own blood. You have nothing to do with the guarantee of the covenant. Your abilities can't strengthen the covenant, and your failures cannot weaken it.

The question is not one of sin, but one of faith. It's not a question of keeping the law, but trusting in God's works. If you are filled with the law, the fruit of the law will produce guilt and condemnation. If you are filled with grace, it will produce life, peace, and the fruit of righteousness.

Trusting in the law is a denial of God's covenant of promise. Trying to keep the law is a denial and disbelief in the fulfillment of Christ. Jesus fulfilled the law. He did not nullify it. God did not break His law, but fulfilled it so the Jews under covenant of the law of Moses and the Gentiles outside the law could both be reconciled to God through Christ. Both those under the law, and those without the biblical law, are in the same spiritual condition. Look at **Romans 2:12**

> For as many as have sinned without law will also perish
> without law, and as many as have sinned in the law will be
> judged by the law

The Fruit of Grace

Nowhere does the Bible say that those outside of the law need to become law-keepers. Romans 3:23 says that all have sinned and fallen short of God's glory. The above passage makes it clear that whether someone is under the law, or outside the law of God, all are under sin's curse. Some perish without the law, while others perish by the judgment of the law. Keep in mind that the Bible says, "If you keep the whole law, but stumble in one point, you are guilty of all the law."[48]

Under the law or not, the answer is the same. The Apostle Paul was a Jewish Pharisee who was changed by the gospel, and became an evangelist to all, but especially to the Gentile world. Look at his ministry in **1 Corinthians 9:20-21**

> [20] and to the Jews I became as a Jew, that I might win Jews; to those *who are* under the law, as under the law, that I might win those *who are* under the law;
> [21] to those *who are* without law, as without law (not being without law toward God, but under law toward Christ), that I might win those *who are* without law;

To the Jews, Paul explained how the law pointed to Christ. To the Gentiles, he preached Christ without teaching the law. The law toward God he called the law of faith,[49] the law of the Spirit of life in Christ,[50] and James called it the law of liberty.[51] It is not the Law of Moses.

To clarify, let's look at the words of Jesus. This passage is often presented to refute the idea that we are under grace and not under the law, yet this passage actually teaches the end of the law. Look at **Matthew 5:17-20**

> [17] "Do not think that I came to destroy the Law or the Prophets. I did not come to destroy but to fulfill.
> [18] "For assuredly, I say to you, till heaven and earth pass away, one jot or one tittle will by no means pass from the

---

[48] James 2:10
[49] Romans 3:27
[50] Romans 8:2
[51] James 2:12

law till all is fulfilled.

19 "Whoever therefore breaks one of the least of these commandments, and teaches men so, shall be called least in the kingdom of heaven; but whoever does and teaches *them*, he shall be called great in the kingdom of heaven.

20 "For I say to you, that unless your righteousness exceeds *the righteousness* of the scribes and Pharisees, you will by no means enter the kingdom of heaven.

I included 19-20 since some teach that being under grace is teaching people to break the law. Of course, unless you were born a Jew, you were never under the Old Testament Law, but even if you were, look at Jesus' words.

He makes it clear that His purpose is not to destroy the law. He wasn't going to break it, annihilate it, or violate the law. He wasn't planning on teaching people to break the law. Yet Jesus makes an interesting statement, "Unless your righteousness exceeds the righteousness of the scribes and Pharisees, you will by no means enter the kingdom of heaven."

When He said these words, he shocked the Jewish people. The Scribes and Pharisees were the pinnacle of human religious achievement. Their entire lives were dedicated to studying the law, interpreting the law, teaching people how to keep the law, and trying to live out the law. There were corrupt Pharisees, such as the ones that condemned Jesus, but many were sincere people trying to live out their faith with their best efforts.

When Jesus said that people had to be more righteous than the scribes and Pharisees, He pushed salvation out of reach of every person in every religious culture. If the most successful and most dedicated religious people were not entering the kingdom, who can? The answer is, "No one. No one that cannot perfectly fulfill the law without committing a single sin."

This takes us back to verses 17 and 18. Jesus came to fulfill the law. To make it clear what this means, He said, "Not one jot or tittle will pass UNTIL all is fulfilled." Jesus did not say the law would never pass away. He said it wouldn't pass away until all is fulfilled.

The Fruit of Grace

And Jesus just stated that He came to fulfill the law. In Christ, the law has come to an end. Those who are in Christ have fulfilled the law by becoming a receiver of Christ's work.

This is why the Gentiles who are outside the law are now righteous in God's sight. Once they are in Christ, they have fulfilled the law. This is also why the Jews who are under the law, who could not enter the kingdom of God because they could never exceed the works of the Pharisees, they are now fulfillers of the law. Once they are in Christ, the law is fulfilled in them. Let's review again this passage in **Romans 8:3-4**

> [3] For what the law could not do in that it was weak through the flesh, God *did* by sending His own Son in the likeness of sinful flesh, on account of sin: He condemned sin in the flesh,
> [4] that the righteous requirement of the law might be fulfilled in us who do not walk according to the flesh but according to the Spirit.

Have you fulfilled the law? That depends on whether you are in Christ. The law is of the flesh, but faith is of the Spirit. If you are in faith, you are a fulfiller of the law. All who are in Christ have fulfilled the righteous requirement of the law.

When you understand these things, it becomes clear why the Bible says, "Without faith it is impossible to please God." We don't please God by how many laws we keep, how many good deeds we do, or how religious we are. God is pleased when you enter into His works by trusting in Christ. If you don't believe God, you will believe you have to keep the law. If you don't believe God, you'll believe you are under condemnation when you stumble.

Good works take care of themselves when we are walking in grace by faith. It was Jesus who said, "I am the vine and you are the branches...if you abide in Me, you will bear much fruit, for without Me, you can do nothing."

Your call is to abide in Christ. It's all about fellowship with God. It's all about your relationship – a love relationship with God, who has expressed unconditional love toward you, and all He asks in return is that you believe in the love He has for you.

Grace does not lead to sin, for the one who trusts in God's grace is focused on Christ and receiving the gifts of the Spirit. Works are what flows out of a heart that is filled with the Spirit. Some claim that teaching grace is to teach people that works don't matter, and this will create apathy. They believe that if we don't have an obligation to work, we won't work.

This also is false. I have a relative who is a retired engineer. He loves the science behind engineering. He is no longer getting paid, but he still works and does the same things he was once employed to do. Hobbyists work hard at their craft because they love it. No one tells a woodworker that they have to build things. They do it because they love it. A golfer works to improve his game because he loves it. Someone who loves to crochet works without any rules demanding her to make something. A gardener loves to work in the garden.

Why do we see people working hard at what they love without anyone lording over them, but we think it's impossible for a heart filled with the love of God to work without a legal requirement to do so? Perhaps Titus 2:11-14 means what God said, that grace teaches us how to deny ungodliness and worldly lusts, teaches us how to live in righteousness, and creates a people of God who are zealous for good works. And this is by grace, not by any requirement of the law. Let's also review **Ephesians 1:6**

To the praise of the glory of His grace, by which He has made us accepted in the Beloved.

You begin from a position of complete acceptance. In Christ, you are acceptable to God and beloved by God. As you learn to trust in grace and walk by faith, the work of the Spirit of grace will begin to bear fruit in your life.

When you stumble, you aren't defeated. Even if you feel like a failure, you are not under God's wrath. Satan will say, "Look at your sin," but God says, "Look at Christ. Trust in My grace."

God does not stand behind you with a rod to strike you when you fall. He is the word of encouragement that tells you not to doubt. You let the flesh distract you, but put your eyes back on Christ. Come confidently before the throne of grace and receive abundant help when you are in need.

If you are like me, you have a lifetime of fleshly mindedness to overcome. When you have a weakness, God calls you to trust in His strength. When you first start walking by faith, you will fall more than you walk. But as you learn to trust in the Spirit and look to Christ, your falls will become less frequent. It's easy to kick yourself, and there is nothing wrong with being sorry for your sins. However, don't doubt God's love and the covenant that secured your forgiveness. You are not trying to get God to forgive you. You are trying to learn to trust in His forgiveness. It's already an accomplished fact.

Every sin you committed in the past was in the future when Jesus purchased your redemption. Every sin you have yet to commit was also purchased at the cross. Once you entered the covenant of promise, your sin was put in the grave – even those you have not yet committed.

Jesus' sacrifice is not bound by time. Ephesians 1:4 says that you were chosen in Christ before the foundation of the world. This is affirmed several times in scripture. A great example is **Revelation 13:8**

All who dwell on the earth will worship him, whose names have not been written in the Book of Life of the Lamb slain from the foundation of the world.

Though this is speaking of those who have not received life, it sheds light to an important truth for us. Jesus didn't begin His work 2000 years ago. God unveiled His eternal work 2000 years ago. God unveiled His invitation to you at the moment in history when He invited you to enter the work He has already accomplished. When you enter the life of the Spirit by faith, you are stepping into God's eternal and timeless work. Then you are outside of the life of the flesh, and life is now about learning how to walk in what has already been accomplished for you.

Your sins are bound to the flesh, but once you step into the Spirit, they are no longer a part of you. There is nothing to overcome. By faith, you are discovering what is yours in the life of the Spirit, and learning how to abide in the eternal. The life of the Spirit can affect your life in the flesh, but the flesh cannot touch the life of the Spirit.

It's time to stop fretting over the weakness of the flesh, and begin trusting in God's power given to you through the Spirit. God has promised that the same Spirit that raised Jesus from the dead is in you, and will give life to your mortal (or physical) body. In other words, your sins have no power. Your flesh cannot defeat you. You are already an overcomer, and as you learn to walk by faith, the life of the Spirit suppresses and defeats any weakness of the flesh.

Your sins cannot defeat the work of Christ. Your failures cannot undo the covenant of Promise. You can't strip the Spirit of its power. You can only choose to trust in the flesh, or trust in the Spirit. You can only choose to walk in the flesh, or walk by faith in the Spirit. You can look at Christ, or look to yourself. You can look at the gift of righteousness through Christ, or look at your own sin.

True obedience is putting your faith in what Christ has done. You can't outgrow your roots. As you become more grounded in Christ, there is no limit to what God has called you to discover. Never stop growing. Never stop learning of Christ. Never stop trusting. Resist looking at your own righteousness or lack thereof. Don't trust in the empty promises of temptation. Every lack has been supplied to those who receive by faith.

May God reveal the power of the Spirit and the revelation of His word to you. Walk by faith, even when you fall short. There is no lack to those who believe. Let's end by reading again the words of **Hebrews 11:6**

> But without faith *it is* impossible to please *Him*, for he who comes to God must believe that He is, and *that* He is a rewarder of those who diligently seek Him.

God delights in giving every good thing to His children. God has hidden all the abundance of His kingdom for you to discover. The more diligently you seek, the more abundantly you find. God gave many good things to Abraham, but the greatest treasure was God Himself. The Lord said to Abraham, "I am your shield and I am your exceedingly great reward."

This promise is also yours. Don't settle for lesser things. Don't be willing to settle for God's provisions or even His promises. Those are blessings, but He is your exceedingly great reward. Everything in God's design is centered around Him revealing Himself to you with the invitation for you to seek Him. God wants you to know Him. As you discover Him, never stop seeking diligently.

Don't let the cares of life crowd out your exceedingly great reward. The more you discover the depth of your relationship with God, the more life will have contentment, the more you'll experience the victorious Christian life, and the more the cares of this life will fade into their rightful place. Don't settle for God helping you escape the problems of life. Learn how to walk on top of the storms with Christ.

You are blessed. You are of the promise. God will never return you to condemnation. When you fall, God asks, "Why did you doubt?" and then He calls you to walk by faith, where success is guaranteed. Experience God!

Discussion Questions

Read Romans 8:3-4 and Hebrews 8:7. What is the difference between the Old Covenant and the New Covenant?

Review Genesis 15:17-18. Why did God not permit Abraham to confirm the covenant of promise?

When Abraham sinned (See Genesis 12:13, Genesis 20:2), why didn't this affect Abraham's covenant?

Read Exodus 24:6-8. Who was the guarantee of the covenant of the law?

Read Deuteronomy 11:26-28. What is the condition for receiving the blessing under the law? What if someone kept most of the law, but stumbled in one area?

Does God call us, who are born in the era of the New Covenant, to go back and submit to the Covenant of the Law in the Old Testament?

Why did God only use Abraham to prepare the sacrifice for the first covenant of promise, but used both Jews and Gentiles to prepare the sacrifice of Christ?

Which covenant are we under? The Covenant to Abraham, the covenant of the law, or the covenant of promise through Christ?

What happens to the New Covenant of Christ when you sin? Is it broken? Why or why not?

Read Matthew 5:17-20, Romans 10:4, and Romans 8:3-4. Did Jesus say that the law would never pass away? Explain your answer based on Matthew 5:17-18.

Has the law come to an end? Why or why not?

How are we fulfillers of the law according to the Bible?

How do we please God?

Does trusting in the completeness of God's grace tempt people to sin? Why or why not?

Does believing in grace, aka hyper-grace, create apathy? Why or why not?

How has this study changed your perspective on your Christian walk?

The Fruit of Grace

If you benefited from this book,
please rate it on Amazon!

Other Recent Books by Eddie Snipes

 The Revelation of Grace. The first book in the Founded Upon Grace Series. Discover the biblical truths that explain the defeat of sin, and the unveiling of our position in Christ!

 The Spirit-Filled Life. The second book in the Founded Upon Grace Series. Discover what it means to walk in the Spirit and to live according to our inner nature, which is always receiving from the Spirit of God.

 Abounding Grace. Is there such thing as hyper-grace? What does the Bible mean by when it says that the grace of Jesus abounded over the sin that came through Adam.

More books from this author:

- It is Finished! Step out of condemnation and into the completed work of Christ.

- The Victorious Christian Life: Living in Grace and Walking in the Spirit.
- The Promise of a Sound Mind : God's plan for emotional and mental health
- Abounding Grace: Dispelling Myths and Clarifying the Biblical Message of God's Overflowing Grace
- Living in the Spirit: God's Plan for you to Thrive in the Abundant Life